Collaboration, Coteaching, and Coaching in Gifted Education

Collaboration, Coteaching, and Coaching in Gifted Education

Gifted Education

Sharing Strategies to Support Gifted Learners

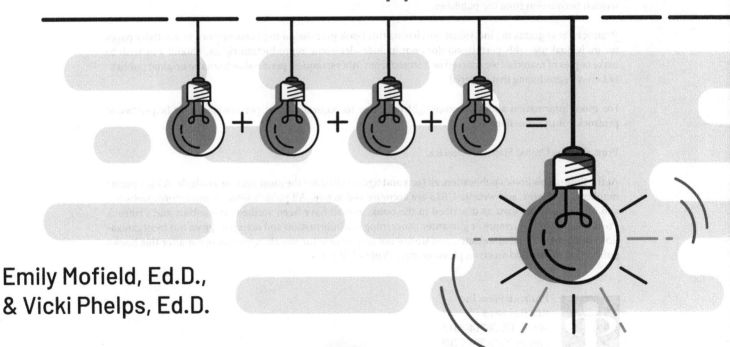

Emily Mofield, Ed.D.,
& Vicki Phelps, Ed.D.

PRUFROCK PRESS INC.
WACO, TEXAS

Prufrock Press Inc.
P.O. Box 8813
Waco, TX 76714-8813
Phone: (800) 998-2208
Fax: (800) 240-0333
http://www.prufrock.com

Dedication

To my beloved husband: Thank you for being my best friend and soulmate through life. To my darling daughter, Ellie: You help me see the extraordinary in the ordinary. To my parents, Bill and Janice: Thank you for always loving me, supporting me, and inspiring me to love learning.

—Emily

To my loving parents, James and Vera Hall: You believed in me before I believed in myself. To my dear children, Brittany, Becca, and David: You continue to inspire me every day. To my incredible husband, David: You are my rock, my confidant, and my strength. Together, we are unstoppable.

—Vicki

Soli deo gloria.

Table of Contents

Acknowledgements

This work is a result from working with many thoughtful, creative classroom teachers and gifted education teachers in Sumner County Schools, Community Unit School District 303, and other schools with whom we have partnered. We value their perspectives on collaborative teaching practices and highlight them throughout the book. Acknowledgement also goes to the Gifted/Multilingual Learners task force between Lipscomb University and Metro Nashville Public Schools. We have learned a great deal from this collaborative endeavor, making strides in identifying and serving gifted students from underrepresented populations, which has also informed our work.

We would also like to thank the Ayers Institute at Lipscomb University (Dr. Rachael Milligan, Dr. Karen Marklein, and Julia Osteen) for their expertise, support, and guidance on instructional coaching. A special thanks goes to Dr. Jessica Novak for her thoughtful suggestions and input on teaching high-potential English language learners. Finally, we want to express our deep appreciation for Katy McDowall, our editor, for her support throughout this exciting journey.

Introduction

This book provides guidance for facilitating productive collaboration within and outside the school for gifted education teachers, specialists, coordinators, coaches, and those in related roles. In the context of educating students with gifts and talents, there are a number of opportunities for collaboration, including:

+ coplanning lessons for differentiation in the regular education classroom,
+ coteaching to provide appropriate levels of challenge for a variety of learners,
+ instructional coaching to activate potential in teachers working with gifted learners,
+ collaborative consultation with a team of educators and professionals to provide specialized supports, and
+ partnering with parents, the community, and outside school agencies to support talent development of students with high potential.

In the context of schools, gifted students often receive most of their instruction in regular education settings, so educators must consider the value of collaboration as an effort to build capacity in teachers' competencies for differentiation. Collaboration through coplanning, coteaching, and instructional coaching with a gifted education teacher or specialist can be an efficient way to build classroom teachers' skills in identifying and challenging gifted learners, ultimately transferring to increased outcomes for student learning. Additionally, through collaboration, gifted education teachers can learn more about academic content used in the regular classroom, thereby connecting it more intently to gifted programming (e.g., pull-out services).

With capacity building as a major goal, we view collaboration as a vehicle for professional learning in the field of gifted education. Best practices in professional learning include models that promote sustained, collaborative, goal-aligned, and transferable active learning (Novak, 2018). Along these lines, collaborative teaching practices and instructional coaching also provide opportunities for reflection, regular follow-up, and positive impact on teacher practices and student learning, as outlined by the National Association for Gifted Children (NAGC) 2019 Gifted Programming Standards (see 6.4.2).

In many school districts, gifted students are served through push-in contexts, in which the gifted education teacher provides instruction within a regular classroom, often in addition to a pull-out setting. Based on our experiences and research on related collaborative teaching models, this book provides a structure for how teachers (gifted education and regular education teachers) can practically approach instructional planning and lesson implementation together, as thinking partners with a shared responsibility for student learning. If teachers are simply tasked with working together without time to thoughtfully plan and reflect, or receive adequate training on the vision, roles, and expectations, this will likely result only in superficial support for students, not meaningful learning. Collaboration can be powerful and rewarding for both students and teachers when defined structures—such as clear protocols, roles and responsibilities, and models for how teachers can navigate collaboration—are in place. Overall, this is the aim of the book, to provide guidance for developing such structures.

Organization of the Book

Chapter 1 defines *collaboration* as an umbrella term and defines various collaborative practices (e.g., coteaching, coaching, collaborative consultation). Collaboration models are presented along a spectrum from simply sharing resources to "colaboring" with others. We present the Collaborative Process Model as a planning guide for all types of collaboration in the book. This model is framed around TEAM (trust, engage, align, maintain), the guiding principles that support sustained, positive, productive collaboration.

Chapter 2 situates collaboration within the context of systemic change. For those at the beginning stages of collaborative teaching, this chapter defines roles and practices, discusses barriers to productive collaboration and how to problem solve through them, provides recommendations for building systems of support for collaboration, and shares lessons learned from recent research (Mofield, 2020b) on teachers' perceptions of benefits and barriers to collaboration.

Chapter 3 delves into the building blocks of coplanning for differentiated instruction. Vertical differentiation is introduced as a way to challenge gifted learners by adding open inquiry, depth, complexity, critical thinking, creative thinking, higher order thinking, abstract thinking, and boundaries to tasks and assignments. We also provide ideas for differentiating assessments and a guide for independent study projects.

Chapter 4 provides the "how" of coplanning. Suggestions are provided for sharing responsibilities, using virtual planning space, and planning long-term units. We also provide a protocol for demonstration teaching (e.g., a gifted education teacher modeling a strategy or portion of a lesson), which allows for reflection on how instructional approaches impact gifted students' learning.

Chapter 5 outlines the adaptation of Friend and Cook's (2017) classic models of coteaching for gifted education. Although the traditional coteaching models are often used to meet the needs of English language learners (ELLs) or students with special needs to enable access to the general curriculum, the adapted models facilitate enrichment or extension to the general curriculum for students who have already mastered the content or need additional challenge.

Chapters 6 and 7 provide summaries and examples of how specific instructional strategies can be used to design lessons with planned "vertical" differentiation. Many of these strategies are tried and true to gifted education, but in these chapters we present them in contexts of working with a classroom teacher through coplanning and coteaching. The strategies in Chapter 6 include overviews of critical and creative thinking process models that can easily be incorporated with content to "tier" a lesson or create a differentiated learning task, and the models in Chapter 7 involve more integrated approaches to the overall lesson design, leading students to deep conceptual understanding.

Chapter 8 introduces instructional coaching in the context of gifted education. We apply the Collaborative Process Model to coaching in order to facilitate effective communication and self-reflection. Instructional coaching activates potential in teachers as they strive to improve their practices around serving and teaching gifted students.

Chapter 9 details a method for collaborative consultation in which the gifted education teacher or specialist works with a team to develop plans to address special needs of gifted learners, particularly twice-exceptionalities, underachievement, and social-emotional concerns. Chapter 10 also provides an overview of specific considerations and supports that can be shared with others pertaining to identifying and serving diverse populations of gifted learners, especially those from culturally, linguistically, and economically diverse backgrounds.

We close in Chapter 11 by expanding the scope of collaboration beyond the walls of the school. We share ideas for promoting parent engagement, using community resources to supplement and enrich academic content, leveraging mentorships to engage students with experts within a specific domain, and partnering with advocacy groups in ways to support gifted education. Through the lens of talent development, we discuss how collaborating with outside agencies and special university programs allows students to learn how experts approach their work in authentic ways, guiding their pursuits of similar paths.

Research Support

What is known about the effects of collaborative teaching as it relates to teaching students with gifts and talents? This is a broad question, and to answer it means considering if the context is coplanning, coteaching, team collaboration, or coaching, as well as the model of service being used (e.g., whether students are in cluster groups in the regular education classroom, or whether the push-in model is used as a supplement to a pull-out model).

Most of what is known about a consultative approach in gifted education is limited to work from the early 2000s, other than a few studies on teachers' perceptions and small case studies. Positive effects have been noted from Landrum (2001), who found that regular education teachers improved their skills in differentiating instruction when a consultative model was used with 10 elementary schools. Known as the catalyst model, the gifted education specialists collaborated with classroom teachers through models like push-in while also providing direct services. Additionally, Masso (2004) found positive effects from coteaching on gifted students' interests and engagement. Few studies in gifted education contexts have examined the effect of coteaching on student achievement. In one report by Wake County Public School System (Lenard & Townsend, 2017), students who were cotaught in science outperformed those who were not cotaught, but these results were not the same for cotaught math and reading classes. Much of the research indicates that administrative support, time for coplanning, and appropriate training on collaborative models are important factors for facilitating effective coteaching. We should note the substantive research on the effectiveness of using cluster grouping of gifted students within regular education classrooms (e.g., Brulles et al., 2012). In this context, there are great possibilities for collaborative teaching in reaching a wide range of learners and making differentiation more manageable for the classroom teacher.

Beyond increasing the classroom teacher's competencies in differentiating, benefits to student learning and engagement are consistently noted in the literature (Landrum, 2001; Lenard & Townsend, 2017; Masso, 2004; Mofield, 2020b). Many of the suggestions in this book are based on findings from Mofield (2020b) revealing teachers' perceived barriers and benefits to collaborative teaching. Using this recent study and recommendations from the coteaching research, we detail the suggestions for effective collaboration (e.g., sufficient planning time, systemic supports, working with volunteers, etc.) in the chapters that follow.

A Starting Point for a Journey

Many of the structures and strategies provided in this book are based on our own successes and challenges of leading teachers in multiple districts and schools (both private and public) through implementing a push-in model as part of a continuum of gifted services. We certainly encountered obstacles along the way but learned many lessons that we are now sharing with you. This book is a user-friendly resource for gifted education teachers and specialists who need practical ideas for making collaboration a meaningful pursuit beyond "being polite and nice" to each other. We hope that you find many of these models and strategies useful, but we also acknowledge you may need to adjust many of these approaches for your specific context. Whether your gifted program adopts an advanced academics approach using Response to Intervention (RtI), a talent development model focused on shaping talent in specific domains, or a model of differentiating content, process, and products as a way to meet the needs of gifted students, the strategies provided in this book can be applied in a variety of contexts aimed to challenge gifted students.

While reading this book, keep in mind that we work from the assumption that all teachers want to help students learn, grow, and develop their potential. We also acknowledge that few teachers have specialized training to address the needs of gifted students (Hertberg-Davis, 2009) and need support in differentiating for the range of abilities and readiness levels among their students. Establishing trust necessary for successful collaboration hinges on relationships and starts with presuming positive intent with collaborative partners (Perkins, 2003). Approaching collaborative work with curiosity, a willingness to grow and learn, and committed spirit to the endeavor will create contexts for success.

This resource may serve only as a starting point on a journey toward productive collaboration. We encourage you to continually grow in your personal efforts in learning more about collaboration and specific models associated with it. Seek out resources, talk to others who have used collaboration successfully, ask questions, and evaluate what is and isn't working. Keep going and keep growing! We encourage you to stay true to the purpose for which collaboration in this context is aimed—to support others in supporting students to understand, show, and grow their gifts and talents.

Chapter 1

The Why, What, and How of Collaboration

Collaboration is the action of working with an individual to produce or create something. The aim, then, is not to simply impart information to a fellow colleague, but to produce ideas together, taking on shared decision making and responsibility for student learning. In the context of this book, we use the term *collaboration* as it relates to the action of a gifted education teacher working with many different professionals to create contexts to identify and nurture students' gifts and talents. We use *collaboration* as an umbrella term encompassing consultation, coplanning, coteaching, and instructional coaching. Collaboration involves working with not only classroom teachers, but also specialists, guidance counselors, parents, community members, advocacy groups, and others. We also recognize that successful collaboration can take place through in-person meetings or online virtual meeting spaces (e.g., Zoom). Regardless of how the collaboration takes place, the principles of strong collaborative practice still hold true.

We view collaboration as a means for capacity building in which other educators and professionals develop skills and knowledge for supporting and challenging gifted learners. Rooted in social constructivist theories, collaboration is a means for individuals to come together in a reflective process and construct new knowledge (Shakenova, 2017). The social interaction and exchange of ideas in the decision-making processes of collaboration lead to new learning and new possibilities. Similarly, through the lens of transformational leadership, collaboration is a way to influence others. In terms of gifted education, this involves influencing educators and others to improve their practices around identifying, teaching, and providing opportunities for students to develop their talents.

Through a variety of models, collaboration can directly facilitate the evidence-based practices tied to the NAGC (2019) Gifted Programming Standards:

+ 6.4.1. Educators regularly reflect on and assess their instructional practices, develop professional learning plans, and improve their practices by participating in continuing education opportunities.
+ 6.4.2. Educators participate in professional learning that is sustained over time, incorporates collaboration and reflection, is goal-aligned and data-driven, is coherent, embedded and transferable, includes regular follow-up, and seeks evidence of positive impact on teacher practice and on increased student learning.

We emphasize that collaboration is an approach that allows two or more individuals to come together to contribute individual expertise to develop shared expertise. The gifted education teacher can share expertise related to understanding and addressing the needs of gifted learners, while a classroom teacher can offer expertise in a content area, which can potentially strengthen links between gifted services and core academic content. These interactions pave the way for opportunities to combine the knowledge, skills, and wisdom of each party to positively affect student learning.

The word *strategies* within the title of this book (*Collaboration, Coteaching, and Coaching in Gifted Education: Sharing Strategies to Support Gifted Learners*) means "a plan of action designed to achieve an overall aim." This is not just a book with instructional approaches for differentiation, but strategies that empower a wide variety of personnel to implement "plans for action" that help develop the strengths and talents of gifted students.

Why Is Collaboration Needed?

Gifted students are gifted all day every day, but often their needs are only addressed for a few hours a week when they attend a gifted enrichment class. Many gifted students spend the majority of their time in the regular classroom, where there is a wide range of academic abilities. Teachers are asked to address the diversity in their classrooms by differentiating for students, which is easier said than done. Collaboration at the classroom level can help alleviate some of the challenges in managing differentiation. Gifted education teachers can collaborate with the classroom teacher to select or develop resources, materials, ideas, and strategies that the classroom teacher can use both now and in the future so that gifted students can learn more advanced content.

Beyond the classroom context, collaboration allows for building understanding about the nature and needs of gifted students among various personnel who are part of a student's education. Through collaboration, some of the issues related to underrepresented populations in gifted programs can be addressed. For example, gifted education teachers may work with administrators, instructional leaders, and ESL (English as a second language) teachers to promote equitable access to gifted programming. Gifted education teachers may work with a guidance counselor to discuss the needs of a gifted student who is chronically underachieving. Collaboration can also occur through community partnerships, opening doors for mentorship possibilities for students who show high potential and interest in a specific domain. As called for by the NAGC (2019) Gifted Programming Standards, gifted educators "regularly engage families and community members for planning, programming, evaluating, and advocating." This can also involve helping families locate community based resources.

We want to emphasize that collaboration is one type of service within a comprehensive coordinated service model. It should exist in conjunction with other types of models, including direct services and specialized programs within a spectrum of services. Landrum (2001) noted, "Collaboration should enhance, rather than diminish, existing school efforts regarding student intervention services. The collaborative process does not eliminate specialized intervention for gifted learners, but rather redefines the roles and responsibilities of school staff in the provision of services" (p. 2). Ultimately, collaboration involves promoting connections between services in multiple areas and can harness the strengths of what each party brings.

Collaboration in Gifted Education: Borrowed From Other Fields

Consultation and collaborative services are models that have been used in other fields, such as special education and ESL programs, for quite some time. In these contexts, collaboration is a means to provide more inclusive services in the general classroom that allow all students access to the regular curriculum. As such, collaboration is a method for closing achievement gaps, but in gifted education, collaboration is a means to develop student strengths and talents by accelerating, enriching, or extending the curriculum. Collaboration in gifted education is based on the idea that all students can make continual progress to the next level of learning, even those who have already mastered grade-level content. Unlike the use of collaboration in other related fields, it is not a means for students to access curriculum, but it is a way to ensure that students continue to be in a stage of learning when interacting with the curriculum. From a talent development perspective, collaboration can also facilitate identifying and strengthening specific talent domains through providing learning opportunities that expose students to "thinking as an expert" within enriched curriculum.

Pull-out programs are a popular model for serving gifted students, but they can be isolated and disconnected from core academics (Landrum, 2001; Treffinger & Selby, 2009). Some districts are incorporating push-in services (to supplement pull-out programs) in which a gifted education teacher provides instruction in the regular education classroom. Doing so allows services to be extended into the regular classroom with more focus on advanced content. It also allows for capacity building for both teachers. Through collaborative teaching, the classroom teacher has opportunities to learn advanced instructional strategies to use with gifted learners, and the gifted education teacher can learn more about the core academic content, incorporating this content within pull-out instruction (Siegle et al., 2019).

What Are the Types of Collaboration?

Collaboration can encompass many different types of interactions between professionals. Throughout this book, we emphasize that these interactions are tools for capacity building, empowering others to better serve gifted students. Collaboration has been defined in gifted education as:

> a style of interaction that includes dialogue, planning, shared and creative decision-making, and follow-up between at least two coequal professionals with diverse expertise, in which the goal of the interaction is to provide appropriate services for students, including high-achieving and gifted students. (Hughes & Murawski, 2001, p. 196)

We define various types of collaboration here:

+ **Consultation:** Consultation is a collaborative effort between the gifted education teacher and other educator where the "consultant" (i.e., gifted education teacher) provides direct guidance to the collaboration partner. In consultation, there is a shift in services from directly working with students to directly working with others who support students.
+ **Coplanning:** Coplanning involves collaboratively developing differentiated instruction, which may or may not lead to coteaching. Coplanning may

involve working together to develop assessments, review assessment data, make decisions for flexible grouping, design tiered assignments, and make other curriculum adaptations.

+ **Coteaching:** Based on Friend and Cook's (2017) conceptualization, co-teaching occurs when two or more professionals share in the responsibility of teaching students within a shared classroom or workplace. It is not a one-teacher classroom with help, but a two-teacher classroom where two individuals are actually *teaching*. Coteaching involves both professionals taking on meaningful roles and usually includes multiple activities taking place within the same space.
+ **Coaching:** Coaching is an ongoing, purposeful collaborative approach to improve teaching and learning through the process of guided reflection.

Benefits of Collaboration

Collaboration brings many benefits for both gifted students and individuals involved in the collaboration process. At the classroom level these benefits include the following (Landrum, 2001; Masso, 2004; Mofield, 2020b):

+ Teaching and recognizing gifted students become shared responsibilities, not just the responsibility of the gifted education teacher.
+ Collaboration allows for harnessing the strengths of each teacher to address students' needs.
+ Classroom teachers learn a repertoire of strategies that they can use with a variety of students.
+ The more knowledge classroom teachers have, the more likely they will use the knowledge to differentiate for students.
+ Gifted education teachers gain opportunities to learn about the regular classroom context and curriculum.
+ Strategies shared by the gifted education teacher can benefit many students in the classroom, not just identified gifted students.
+ Gifted pull-out programs can feel isolated; collaboration allows for more direct links to the regular curriculum (i.e., pull-out instruction can tie in content from the regular classroom).
+ Collaboration enhances trust and facilitates communication about the needs of gifted students.
+ Working with others is a way to ignite advocacy efforts.
+ Collaboration allows for various points of view that both parties bring to "enable instruction to be richer, deeper, and tailored to each student's needs" (Friend, 2016, p. 6).

+ Increased teacher skills can translate to better student outcomes.
+ When two or more come together, combined efforts create innovative ways to help all learners.

Barriers

Although there are many benefits to collaboration, a number of barriers prevent it from being successful and sustainable (Haberlin, 2016; Mofield, 2020b; Scruggs et al., 2007). In understanding barriers, you may proactively work to consider how to address them through system structures, careful communication, and intentional program planning. Barriers include:

+ It is difficult for both parties to find common planning time.
+ Many assumptions need to be addressed. Gifted education teachers could think, "I know best," while classroom teachers may assume they are already meeting the needs of all students in their classrooms. Classroom teachers could also view the gifted education teacher as taking an evaluative or judgmental role in the collaborative context.
+ Many classroom teachers are not aware of the unique needs of gifted students. Misconceptions about their needs can prevent classroom teachers from welcoming collaboration with gifted education teachers.
+ It can take a long time to develop positive working relationships for collaboration.
+ There can be considerable frustration when parties have different ideas, opinions, and styles for teaching students.
+ Collaboration alone through coteaching or coplanning may not be intensive enough to meet the needs of gifted students.

How Does This Work? The Collaborative Process Model

Collaboration is more than cooperating with each other or "playing nicely" with one another. In order for collaboration to lead to deep professional learning and productive outcomes, collaborators must work toward achieving shared goals in the context of respect and trust. Cooperation involves providing basic assistance to a colleague, whereas collaboration necessitates shared values and shared decision making about teacher practices (Kruse, 1999). Collaboration can remain superficial and shallow when teachers are reluctant to engage in the process because they have been "volun-told" to do so by administrators. To avoid such cases, collaboration must take place in a culture that supports it; where flexibility, creativity, and risk-taking are encouraged; and where structural conditions, such as time to coplan, observe, and reflect together, are intentionally arranged (Shakenova, 2017).

As mentioned previously, collaboration comes out of social constructivism: New knowledge is coproduced from the sharing of ideas. Additionally, research on collaboration in both leadership and education provides guidance on the structural conditions and interpersonal dynamics that facilitate productive collaboration. We have taken these components and incorporated them into a user-friendly model (see Figure 1) that can be used in various forms of collaboration. Resource 1: Collaborative Process Model can be used to engage in conversations about each component.

Develop Shared Understanding

First, the team members must understand that collaboration will involve a shared course of action in which each individual contributes in decision making and reflection along the way. This means setting the stage for what is expected in collaboration in terms of roles and what to do. The collaborative team should have open dialogue about the following:

+ expectations during the collaboration (including norms, expected roles and responsibilities, timelines, etc.);
+ steps of the collaborative process (set a purpose, plan, and reflect) and structural conditions that support it (when, where, and how to collaborate); and
+ interpersonal dynamics of collaboration (TEAM frame: trust, engage, align, and maintain).

In the chapters that follow, we provide guidance on the first component—establishing expectations, roles, responsibilities, and mutually established norms for various collaborative practices. Steps of the collaborative process and interpersonal dynamics are further explained in the following sections.

Steps of the Collaborative Process

The Collaborative Process Model is meant to be flexible and apply to various forms of collaboration: coplanning, coteaching, coaching, and consultation. Table 1 provides questions to consider for each step of the process to establish guidance for sharing dialogue and exchanging ideas for new learning. Collaborators should also determine structural conditions that best facilitate moving through these steps,

FIGURE 1
Collaborative Process Model

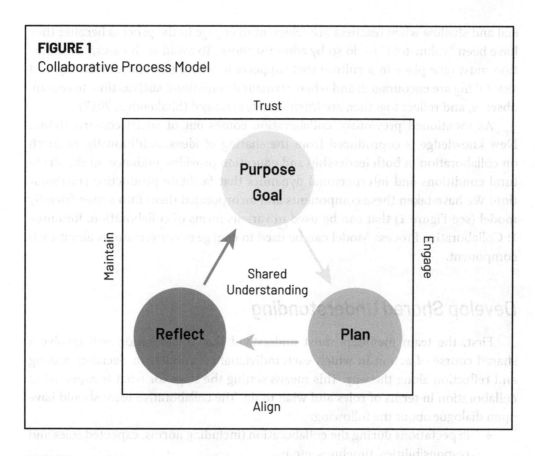

TABLE 1
Collaborative Steps and Questions to Consider

Collaborative Steps	Questions to Consider
Set a Purpose	+ What is our goal? What do we seek to do, specifically? + What are our desired outcomes? + What is our main goal for the meeting?
Plan	+ How will this be done? + Who will do what? + What resources will we need? + What strategies will we use?
Reflect	+ Did we accomplish our purpose and goal? + What worked, and what didn't work? + What are our next steps in moving forward?

	Shared Understanding	
	What expectations do we have of each other through the process of collaboration? How do we approach the components below? What are our norms? How do we define our roles?	

	Trust	
	How will we intentionally develop trust (e.g., presume positive intent, respect opinions even if we disagree, follow through on tasks, provide honest feedback, strive for balanced contribution, follow through on established norms)?	

Maintain	**Steps: Shared Decision Making**	**Engage**
Do we feel comfortable with the process so far?	1. **Set a Purpose:** What is our goal? What will be our focus?	What are my own strengths and weaknesses?
Is there anything we need to revisit or change in working together?	2. **Plan:** What is our plan? Who will do what? When and how will we do this? What do we need?	What strengths do we see in each other?
(Revisit throughout, ongoing.)	3. **Reflection:** What worked? What did not work? What if we___? What are next steps for students? What new knowledge do we now have?	How will we apply our strengths?

	Align	
	What are my underlying assumptions about this process? What are my core beliefs about student learning, particularly with gifted students? How do we align our teaching styles . . . our philosophies . . . our values?	

Note. Created by E. Mofield and V. Phelps.

specifically considering time, place, and context (e.g., observing a lesson, developing materials, working together to develop a specialized intervention, etc.).

1. **Set a purpose:** During the collaborative process, start with the desired goal. Ask, "What do we seek to do, specifically?" One barrier to successful collaboration can be lack of clear communication. A clear purpose should be set for the collaborative meeting. For example, the gifted education teacher and classroom teacher's purpose in collaboration might be to review preassessments in order to develop differentiated plans for flexible groups. Teams that decide upon and define their goals together are more effective in their collaborative efforts (Friend & Cook, 2017).

2. **Plan:** The purpose should then drive the plan through the sharing of ideas, experiences, and resources. During the planning stage, shared decisions are made relating to how the goal is to be achieved and who will implement which parts of the plan. In our example, this may include decisions regarding questions, such as "Which students showed mastery of content already? What strategies will be used in the flexible groups? What evidence will we collect for student learning?" The plan is then implemented.

3. **Reflect:** Reflecting on the plan, how it was implemented, and the collaborative process itself sets the stage for the construction of new knowledge. Through reflection comes self-awareness, insight into teaching practices, and potential for improved practice. Teams should deliberately plan to embed this important component, as reflection ignites "change" in individuals, particularly in terms of how they approach instructional practice.

This model is meant to provide a structure that can help colleagues move from simply talking about ideas to engaging in deeper levels of professional learning. This occurs when each member makes meaningful contributions in decision making. Individual growth happens through such interactive dialogue and active participation. These steps, however, must be approached within the parameters of positive interpersonal dynamics, factors that especially influence the effectiveness of teacher collaboration: trust, open communication, shared beliefs and understanding, and respect (Shakenova, 2017). These factors are embedded around the collaborative process steps through the frame of TEAM—trust, engage, align, and maintain.

TEAM Frame

Collaboration is a complex interpersonal process that must be established on the foundation of trust, reciprocity, and respect (Matthews et al., 2007). Here, we offer a model for authentic communication that can be used as the groundwork for collaborative relationships. We refer to this throughout the book for developing positive dialogue and reflection about the collaborative process as the TEAM frame (Mofield, 2020b; see Figure 2):

+ **T—Trust:** Instill a sense of trust with one another. Develop a positive, caring relationship that allows for risk-taking and honesty in giving feedback on how collaboration is working. Give trust to get trust. In establishing trust, remember trust assumes that the partner's intentions are good (e.g., presuming positive intent).

+ **E—Engage:** Engage each other in the planning process, valuing the expertise of each. Ask questions, listen to ideas, and build from one another's ideas. Offer encouragement and praise. Engage to actively address unspoken assumptions of each party.

+ **A—Align:** Align beliefs for student discipline, teaching style, and expectations of all parties. Openly discuss each other's values (e.g., accelerating content, aligning lessons to student interests) and be willing to work toward an "and" rather than "or" approach to shared decision making.

+ **M—Maintain:** Maintain a positive relationship through frequent reflective discussions on what has worked and what has not worked. Be open to feedback about what could be improved and what you may try next time. Provide descriptive rather than evaluative feedback and avoid being judgmental. This component should be ongoing, to be visited throughout the collaborative task.

Spectrum of Collaboration

Collaboration can be organized along a spectrum with increased levels of shared responsibility to address the needs of gifted learners. The spectrum of collaboration is shown in Table 2.

Under the category "Sharing Resources," we include ways the gifted education teacher can share strategies with others. At this level, the gifted education teacher may not directly engage with the classroom teacher in *shared* decision making. These methods include simply imparting ideas and information through email communication and grade-level meetings, demonstrating a strategy for a classroom teacher, or sharing information with parents. The next level involves coteaching, coplanning, or coaching, which includes working with another teacher or professional to share in the responsibility of developing and/or delivering differentiated instruction. With other professionals, this may involve coplanning an intervention for twice-exceptional students or consulting with an ESL teacher to share in data collection for a gifted screening process. Then, the next level is Team Problem Solving.

FIGURE 2
TEAM Frame for Collaboration

T	Trust
E	Engage Each Other's Expertise
A	Align Beliefs and Values
M	Maintain the Relationship

TABLE 2
A Spectrum of Collaboration

Increased Collective Collaboration With Others →		
Sharing Resources	**Coplanning, Coteaching, and Coaching**	**Team Problem Solving**
+ Emailing resources + Sharing online resources + Providing professional learning about the needs of gifted students + Participating in professional learning communities + Demonstrating a strategy for a classroom teacher + Presenting information at parent meetings	+ Coplanning a lesson with tiered instruction + Virtual coplanning (shared plan books) + Applying methods of coteaching in the classroom + Working directly with specialists (e.g., ESL teachers) who share their expertise in coplanning + Coaching a teacher through reflective practice	+ Working in collaborative team meetings with various personnel + Consulting with a team to consider specialized interventions + Collaborating in Individualized Education Program (IEP) meetings + Identifying students for gifted services + Working with community organizations and universities to plan extended programming

This involves a collaborative team addressing special student issues or developing broad plans to provide support or programming.

True collaboration involves the *coaction* of both parties being involved in decision making. Sharing resources through email or a shared electronic drive is the action of only one teacher assisting another colleague. Simply sharing resources does not allow for both individuals to engage in dialogue or make decisions together.

However, the sharing of resources can eventually lead to more interactive collaboration efforts in which the classroom teacher is more involved in the process. Thus, the approaches under "Sharing Resources" in Table 2 can serve as an invitation for future collaboration efforts.

Is This Pie in the Sky?

We acknowledge that collaboration is not easy work. It involves complexities of working with other individuals with different beliefs, values, and assumptions. It can involve conflict and can even feel awkward or uncomfortable. Ultimately, collaboration requires the courage to go beyond your own comfort zone, reaching out to not only listen, but also value the ideas of others. So, does this really work? The answer to this question depends on levels of support, type of collaborative culture, attitudes of those involved, clarity of collaboration's vision and purpose, and level of commitment each partner is willing to make to the process. Overall, collaboration can be rewarding and powerful for both teachers and students. Collaborating teachers benefit from active learning, ongoing reflection, and new personal knowledge, while students benefit from challenging and engaging instruction aimed to develop their gifts and talents. The key to making collaboration work hinges on relationships, and so, we emphasize the use of the TEAM frame (trust, engage, align, and maintain) as a strong foundation for supporting this work.

Chapter 2

Preparing a Path for Successful Collaboration

This chapter focuses on the first steps of collaboration within the school context. Implementing collaboration at the classroom level (e.g., modeling a strategy, coplanning with a classroom teacher, coteaching, etc.) does not happen overnight, nor is it an easy endeavor. It requires a long-term commitment from administrators, program directors, and all personnel involved in the process. Implementing collaborative teaching can take a considerable amount of time and can involve working with others who may have different teaching styles and philosophies. Further, without supportive structures (e.g., adequate training on the vision, roles, and expectations of collaboration; time to thoughtfully plan and reflect together; etc.) collaboration will likely result in only superficial support for students, not meaningful learning. So, where do you begin?

Communicating Collaboration

Collaborators must consider the important question "How does collaboration facilitate learning?" To engage all parties in this question, the purpose of collaboration should be clearly defined within the gifted programming model. What is the vision and philosophy of the gifted program? What are the program goals? How does collaboration help achieve these goals? What is the role of the gifted education teacher (e.g., do gifted education teachers serve as coteachers within a push-in model to supplement and connect pull-out programming to academic content?)? Referring to the Collaborative Process Model (see Figure 1, p. 14), it is important to always begin with the purpose and desired outcome for the collaborative endeavor and articulate it so that everyone understands the focus.

The vision, purpose, and plan for supporting collaboration need to be clearly communicated to school faculty. In our experiences, this works best when building administrators express their support by articulating the importance and value of collaboration. Administrators might pose the question, "What are we doing to help high-ability students continue to make academic progress?" The administrator can solicit input from various perspectives and connect it to how collaboration can help teachers manage differentiation in meeting the needs of all students.

Sharing the types of collaborative roles should be communicated to all school personnel (see Table 1, p. 14). For classroom-based collaboration the gifted education teacher might explain that they can share resources online through a virtual platform, model a high-level thinking strategy, coplan lessons, coteach in the classroom, or perhaps act as an instructional coach (if the gifted education teacher serves in that capacity).

Professional Learning

If classroom-based collaboration is an expected model of service for gifted students (e.g., push-in coteaching, coplanning, etc.), those involved must engage in professional learning in order to grow in this practice. The district should provide professional learning opportunities to set the stage for introducing the vision, purpose, and structures for collaboration, including differentiation strategies to be used. Further opportunities for practice, reflection, feedback, and ongoing collegial support are needed to sustain collaborative practice. Although it seems obvious, both the gifted education teacher and collaborative partner (e.g., classroom teacher) should attend formal training and other ongoing professional learning about collaboration/coteaching together. Table 3 offers suggestions for what districts might include in sessions for initial training and ongoing professional learning for those involved in collaborative work.

We should emphasize that receiving information during a training is not likely to translate into action unless the components of theory, demonstration, practice, feedback, and collegial support are present (Joyce & Showers, 2002). Often presenters share theory and justification for a new method and demonstrate how skills are to be used in practice; however, teachers also need the opportunities to actually

TABLE 3
Topic Ideas for Initial Training and Ongoing Professional
Learning on Collaborative Practices

Rationale	+ The why and what of differentiation for gifted learners + How collaboration facilitates differentiation
Collaboration in Gifted Education	+ Overview of the spectrum of services for gifted students + Overview of different types of collaboration + Presentation of clear vision and purpose of collaboration in context of gifted education (e.g., identify and serve gifted students in regular education) + Role of gifted education teacher and classroom teacher
Collaborative Process Model and Building Relationships	+ Collaborative Process Model and TEAM frame (trust, engage, align, and maintain) + Practice developing a "mini" plan applying the Collaborative Process Model (e.g., codevelop plan for preassessment enrichment activities)
Understanding Assumptions	+ Reflection on personal assumptions + Reflection on assumptions and perspectives of each partner + SCARF model examining threats and enhancers to relationships (described later in chapter)
Coteaching (If Applicable)	+ Introduction to coteaching models + Practice opportunities for coaction (e.g., coplanning a lesson together, coteaching a small portion of a lesson) with actionable feedback
Strategies	+ Introduction and application of strategies for differentiation through coplanning + Common language for differentiation
Ongoing Practice and Reflection	+ Ongoing feedback to collaborative partners on practice opportunities during training as well as in collaborative contexts + Built-in time for teachers to reflect on their professional learning and plan for next steps + Collegial support in small groups for collaborators to reflect on goals and share successes and failures

practice applying the news skills (e.g., coplanning for differentiation, coinstructing, etc.). Ongoing professional learning should include opportunities for giving and receiving specific feedback. For example, partner teachers may video-record themselves while coteaching and share these videos in a learning community where feedback can be shared. Follow-up with collegial support includes providing opportunities for small groups to share resources, reflect, and determine next steps for collaboration (Murawski & Lochner, 2018). In the context of gifted education, we suggest having regular opportunities for partnered gifted education teachers and regular education teachers to come together in communities of practice for this ongoing support.

One-day "sit-and-get, whew—I'm through" professional development will not result in sustained practices. As emphasized in the Every Student Succeeds Act (ESSA, 2015), professional development should be "sustained, intensive, collaborative, job-embedded, data-driven, and student-focused." Therefore, professional learning must harness buy-in for those involved. This can be established by creating a vision for success, "What does it look like for us to achieve successful collaboration?" As teaching partners actively engage in reflection in ongoing learning communities around collaborative practices, they can identify specific skills to improve collaboration. For example, they can focus on refining a specific skill in their collaborative practice (e.g., focus on developing and using assessment to inform instruction; Murawski & Lochner, 2018). This type of job-embedded professional learning leads to sustained change.

Defining Roles and Understanding Assumptions

Professional learning sessions should emphasize the shared responsibility in collaboration and provide opportunities to define roles. Specifically, in order to support differentiation, the gifted education teacher's role might be to develop preassessments, modify curricula, work with groups who need more challenging instruction, model use of higher order thinking questions, or work one-on-one with students. The classroom teacher's role may be to share the weekly instructional objectives aligned with standards and provide initial ideas for learning activities. Table 4 provides examples of possible roles for each teacher. We want to emphasize, however, that these roles are fluid and may not necessarily be done separately by each teacher. For example, although the gifted education teacher may have the primary role in developing a tiered assignment, both teachers may work together on this so that the classroom teacher also learns the skill of developing tiered assignments.

In defining roles, you must also examine personal assumptions and consider the assumptions of others. For example, the gifted education teacher may work from an implicit assumption that instruction in the regular classroom is insufficient to meet the needs of gifted students. Classroom teachers may assume that they do not need support in differentiation because they are already meeting the needs of high-ability students. Covey's (1989/2015) advice, "seek first to understand," can go

TABLE 4
Ideas for Roles and Responsibilities

Roles of the Gifted Education Teacher	Shared Roles	Roles of the Classroom Teacher
+ Provide support to develop differentiated tiered assignments aligned to instructional goals + Differentiate station activities with high-level tasks + Develop higher order questions that can be asked during instruction + Modify assessments and develop differentiated rubrics that extend ceilings	+ Develop preassessments that assess for student knowledge *and* conceptual understanding of the content + Work to ensure each student is learning and is challenged + Understand the different learning profiles and needs of students + Make decisions on flexible grouping	+ Share content knowledge + Develop and share initial lesson plans with gifted teacher + Develop instructional goals (what students should know, do, and understand) based on standards + Develop initial ideas for learning activities and tasks to attain instructional goals + Develop assessments and rubrics

a long way in addressing underlying belief systems and assumptions of each individual. The gifted education teacher may need to explain that they are not there to tell the classroom teacher what to do and that the classroom teacher has not done anything "wrong" to need support. A clear purpose for collaboration must be articulated: to work together to promote continuous progress of learning for all students. Understanding and moving past assumptions at the beginning of collaborative relationships can propel the team to move beyond a superficial operation of collaboration toward an authentic relationship.

Volunteer Participation

Volunteer participation from both parties is a nonnegotiable for collaboration to work (Scruggs et al., 2007). If collaboration at the classroom level is a new model for a school district, accept that some teachers are not open to another teacher modeling a strategy in their classrooms, and they especially may be resistant to coteaching. In the beginning stages, gifted education teachers can focus on working with a few open and willing classroom teachers who are viewed as leaders or influencers within the school (Mofield, 2020b). Start working with the teachers who are eager and excited to learn new strategies and who will likely share about positive collaboration experiences with others. Focus on a few teachers within a school rather than try to work with multiple teachers sporadically. Servicing students through an indirect consultation model requires consistency; otherwise, students may receive only small doses of differentiation.

Schedules and Cluster Grouping

Setting up the right contexts for scheduling is important. A set schedule of collaborating with a teacher at least once per week on a regular basis (e.g., a minimum of 30 minutes of coplanning per week) provides a stronger dose of service than intermittently working with teachers once or twice per semester.

It can be a logistical nightmare for a gifted education teacher to work with multiple teachers when gifted students are dispersed in multiple classrooms. Cluster grouping is also a way to provide environments in which gifted students are with like-ability peers in the regular classroom. Typically, clusters include 8–15 students of similar ability placed with students within a heterogeneous classroom. Cluster grouping allows the gifted education teacher to collaborate with a smaller number of teachers. We recommend the use of a cluster grouping model, such as the Total School Cluster Grouping Model (TSCG; Gentry & Mann, 2009), to guide decisions about cluster placements. The TSCG model emphasizes the use of both teacher identification and achievement test results to nominate students into clusters (high achieving, above-average achieving, average achieving, low-average achieving, and low achieving). Then, students are placed into classrooms based on these data. Table 5 shows a possible placement of students into classrooms.

Define Differentiation Frameworks

Providing a clear framework and common language for differentiation (to be discussed in Chapter 3) is important. This is the opportunity to provide clear definitions and examples of words, such as *depth*, *complexity*, and *rigor*. Providing models for critical thinking (e.g., Paul and Elder's [2019] elements of reasoning) can facilitate and equip teachers to build in high-level processing into questions, tasks, and assignments. Also, using a consistent model for gifted curriculum can provide a structure for coplanning units and lesson plans between gifted education teachers and classroom teachers. For example, using the Integrated Curriculum Model (ICM; VanTassel-Baska & Baska, 2019) can help teachers intentionally differentiate

TABLE 5
Student Cluster Assignment by Classroom

	Total	Classroom 1	Classroom 2	Classroom 3	Classroom 4	Classroom 5
High Achieving	17	14[1]	3			
Above-Average	17		7	4	0	6
Average	55	8	14	9	16	8[2]
Low-Average	20	3	4	5	0	8
Low	14	0	0	7	7	0
Special Education	5	1[1]				4[2]
Total	123	25	28	25	23	22

Note. The special education category does not count toward the total, as these students are already counted in their respective achievement category. Adapted from *Beyond Gifted Education: Designing and Implementing Advanced Academic Programs* (p. 82), by S. J. Peters, M. S. Matthews, M. T. McBee, and D. B. McCoach, 2013, Prufrock Press. Copyright 2013 by Prufrock Press. Adapted with permission.

1 Twice-exceptional child who is gifted and has a learning disability
2 Students with a disability who are also average achieving

by addressing advanced content and advanced processes, and tying content to an overarching concept or issue. With a common language and structure, curriculum modifications are more likely to be made with thoughtful intentions rather than randomly.

Nonnegotiables

In order for collaboration to be successful, especially as applied to classroom-based collaboration, a number of nonnegotiables are recommended from historical literature (i.e., Landrum, 2001) on collaborative practices in gifted education. Many of these nonnegotiables also surfaced within a more recent research study on teachers' perceptions of collaboration (Mofield, 2020b):

1. Use a flexible pace of instruction.
2. Use flexible student grouping.
3. Plan regularly (both short-term and long-term planning).
4. Collaborate with volunteer participants.
5. Provide professional learning.
6. Have administrative support.
7. Document consultative activities.
8. Have a low ratio of gifted teachers to number of collaborative colleagues.
9. Value the input of both parties, each with their own expertise.
10. Ensure students have continued support for direct service from a trained gifted teacher.

Without these supports, sustaining successful collaboration over time is more difficult. These nonnegotiables should be clearly communicated to all individuals involved, and administrators and program directors should carefully develop infrastructures to facilitate these supports over time.

Removing Interpersonal Threats in Collaboration: SCARF

The interpersonal dynamics in collaboration—such as listening, nurturing trust, and making decisions together—often require risk-taking and vulnerability. The process of collaboration is not always a comfortable one, especially if an individual feels judged, controlled, and disconnected, or perceives unfairness and uncertainty. Rock (2008) provided a framework for understanding areas that influence people's behaviors in social situations; these influences can pose as threats or as enhancers in the relationship. The coactions of problem solving, coplanning, and coteaching are difficult to pursue and implement if an individual feels threatened. Rooted in neuroscience, Rock explained these domains through the acronym SCARF, which can be especially useful in effectively working with others.

As defined by Rock (2008), SCARF stands for:

+ **S—Status:** Your relative importance to others.
+ **C—Certainty:** Your ability to predict the future.
+ **A—Autonomy:** Your sense of control over events.
+ **R—Relatedness:** How safe you feel with others.
+ **F—Fairness:** How fair you perceive the exchanges between people to be.

This framework is applicable in any collaborative work, and so, collaborative teams might consider intentionally addressing each element in order to eliminate threats in relationships.

Status

What can you do to ensure that collaborative partners think, "I am respected and others think positively of me"? The words you use in conversation have a profound effect on a person's perception of self-status. Words can evoke defensiveness or a sense of empowerment. For example, a gifted education teacher asking a classroom teacher, "Can I give you some suggestions for strategies to use in your classroom?" might convey an assumption that the classroom teacher does not already use appropriate strategies. The question assumes that the teacher needs help and that the gifted education teacher is the "hero" to save the day. The simple question can be a threat to the person's status.

Instead, collaborators should strive for considering language with positive intent. For example, instead of posing a question that assumes the classroom teacher does not use effective strategies (e.g., "Have you tried to use differentiation with your gifted students?"), ask, "What strategies are you using with your gifted students?" This, instead, assumes that the classroom teacher is thinking about all learners in their class and has considered a variety of approaches to enhance student learning. Then, the classroom teacher may ask the gifted education teacher about strategies, leading to open communication and collaboration. Table 6 provides example stems that might reflect presumed positive intent in contrast to questions that provide threats and defensive attitudes.

Certainty

Consider how providing certainty can relieve threats within collaboration. What can you do to ensure that boundaries and expectations are set at the start? As previously discussed, clarifying roles, responsibilities, and establishing norms for all types of collaboration will enhance clear expectations. The structures of the Collaborative Process Model and the interpersonal components of the TEAM frame can pave the path to certainty. All collaborators will know what to expect because the components are discussed up front. Such structures take the guesswork out of what each collaborator is supposed to do and what the collaboration involves.

TABLE 6
Presuming Positive Intent

Instead of	Consider
+ Have you . . . ? + Could you . . . ? + Do you . . . ? + Can you . . . ?	+ What . . . ? + Which . . . ? + As someone who . . . ? + When . . . ? + In what ways . . . ? + Given . . . ?
Have you thought about why the student is acting out in your class?	Given what we know about characteristics of gifted students, what characteristics and behaviors are you seeing?

Note. Adapted from Kee et al. (2010).

Autonomy

Students' motivation increases when they are given choices and opportunities to make decisions for themselves; this is also true, if not more so, for adults. During collaboration, rather than continually offering suggestions and strategies, the sharing of strategies should be pursued as an invitation to the teacher. The gifted education teacher might ask, "Would you mind if we brainstorm some ideas together?" After including the classroom teacher's input, then the gifted education teacher may invite the classroom teacher to have more autonomy over the instructional approaches by asking, "Which one of these strategies would we like to try?" This approach allows the classroom teacher to have a sense of control in decision making by promoting shared responsibility.

Relatedness

Relatedness is built through personal connections and seeking commonalities among collaborators. Certainly, building relationships is foundational to lasting, trusting relationships. Relatedness is often built from other aspects of the SCARF model. When a person feels valued and respected by another individual, this, of course, enhances relatedness. When roles, responsibilities, and expectations are clarified through "certainty," this also establishes a safe environment for building relationships.

Fairness

The perception of fairness can make or break collaborative relationships. When people perceive they are not treated equally, this undermines trust and other parts of the SCARF model (e.g., status, certainty). For example, some classroom teachers might perceive that gifted education teachers work with the "smartest" kids, which "must be an easy job." Fairness is achieved when team members are vulnerable and transparent. Further, like with certainty, clear roles, responsibilities, and shared norms also establish fairness.

When a teacher is not open to collaboration, one or more of these components may be functioning as threats within the relationship. For example, a classroom teacher might feel a threat to a sense of control (autonomy) regarding a change in regular routine classroom practices from coteaching, or perhaps, a classroom teacher feels that status is threatened if it is perceived they need "help" from the gifted education teacher to support gifted learners.

Easing In

Depending on the context, it may be up to the gifted education teacher to initiate collaboration efforts within the school. How do you ease into a collaborative role, and what are the very first steps to take? First, get to know teachers in the school. Often gifted teachers serve multiple schools and grade levels, which makes it difficult to build relationships with other staff. Eating lunch with teachers, participating in faculty meetings, and regularly being present in school activities can go a long way in developing the foundations of positive relationships. These are ways for you to know what is happening in the regular classroom and explain what services you provide, from sharing resources and coteaching to problem solving through more complex issues with a student. Communicating your role in the school can also be accomplished through an introductory email, a survey, or providing notes in mailboxes (of course, chocolate can go a long way, too!).

As you think about more long-term collaborative partners, consider: Who will be open to coplanning? Who will be open to coteaching? For many classroom teachers, differentiation through collaboration is a paradigm shift. If you have the opportunity to choose who to work with, it can be easier to work closely with classroom teachers who already have experience with collaboration or who are eager to jump on board. This might even include teachers new to the profession. Be sure that collaboration is an invitation, not a mandate for the teacher.

Preparing for successful collaboration also involves learning the context and culture of the school. Take time to browse the hallways of the school and notice the work displayed. This can provide insight into the curricular content and can pave the way for you to invite collaboration by developing resources or extension activities for a unit. Teachers may be open to this level of invitational collaboration (sharing resources) before committing to more involved collaboration, such as coplanning or coteaching.

Another way to ease into collaboration is to ask teachers if you can observe students in their classrooms. You can learn about the teacher's style, the classroom culture, and content, which can lead to opportunities for sharing resources, modeling a strategy, or coplanning a differentiated lesson. Attending grade-level meetings and professional learning communities (PLCs) to become familiar with the grade-level content and curriculum can also show other classroom teachers that you are intentional about supporting or coplanning instruction relevant to standards.

If teachers are reluctant to collaborate, you can also use opportunities to discuss problems or issues they are having with gifted students as a way to open the door for collaboration. For example, a teacher may discuss with you that a student displays disruptive behavior or is underachieving. You may offer to observe the student in the classroom context. In a follow-up meeting, you might offer suggestions for curricular modifications that may address issues related to boredom and motivation. Through this consulting process, the classroom teacher may want to continue to seek out support through more deliberate classroom collaboration.

Beyond collaborating to coplan instruction for the regular education classroom, the gifted education teacher may also collaborate with the classroom teacher in order to more intentionally connect academic core content to other areas of gifted programming (e.g., pull-out services). This tighter link between regular education and gifted education programming can potentially allow for even deeper learning as students study extensions to advanced content.

We have also found it helpful to start with sharing resources and modeling a strategy in a classroom before moving toward more involved collaboration (coplanning and coteaching). For example, you may have more success in building a collaborative relationship if you can start by modeling a strategy for a short portion of a lesson a couple of times in a classroom. Keep in mind that it takes time to get the ball rolling with successful collaboration. Over time, you may need to request for continued administrative support to ensure collaboration is an accountable and sustainable practice.

Administrative Support

Proactive support from administrators is key to promoting successful collaboration, so what are some first steps in talking with administrators about supporting the role of classroom collaboration as a service to gifted learners? Administrators are often accustomed to teachers and parents coming to them with problems that need to be solved. In the discussions about collaboration, you can be equipped with solutions relating to the needs of gifted students. Often, when student data are discussed, administrators ask, "What are we doing to promote the growth of our highest achieving students?" or "Why are our gifted students not growing academically?" A rationale for classroom collaboration between classroom teachers and gifted education teachers can be presented as a way to increase overall achievement.

If the district is introducing classroom collaboration through a model such as push-in services (as a supplement to pull-out services), you can offer support to administrators in managing and implementing the model in their school. Schedule a time to meet with administrators about the benefits and the barriers to successful collaboration, which include scheduling issues. During this meeting, you may also emphasize the value of a cluster group model that would enable a gifted education teacher to work intentionally with a few teachers. The administrators may make decisions regarding which teachers will teach the gifted cluster groups, or perhaps which teachers will be good candidates for coteaching with the gifted education teachers. These conversations need to happen early so that administration can have time to sufficiently plan and schedule. Also remember that time for coplanning should be deliberately scheduled within a master schedule. To prepare for scheduling, questions to consider might be the following: How many teachers will the gifted education teacher work with on a regular basis? In what grade levels will this happen? What students will be in these classes? Will the gifted education teacher primarily coplan with this teacher or also coteach?

The following are important factors for administrators to consider in promoting successful collaboration:

+ Develop an appropriate master schedule that allows for coplanning on a regular basis. In order for teachers to work together, they must have time to do so. Consider which classroom teachers and grade levels are most suitable for collaboration with the gifted education teacher.

+ Plan student grouping to minimize the number of classrooms in which the gifted education teacher coplans or coteaches.

+ Provide and support professional learning related to all forms of collaboration. Provide incentives for teachers who participate.

+ Emphasize to faculty that collaboration can enhance not only gifted students' learning, but other students' learning as well.

+ Provide opportunities for long-term planning days when teachers can map out plans for the year.

+ Provide resources and tools to support differentiation within the classroom. Equipping teachers with appropriate resources can help them pursue their own efforts for differentiation beyond the collaboration with the gifted education teacher.

+ Articulate the importance of differentiation. Give teachers permission to not stay tied to a scripted curriculum or pacing guide. Emphasize that each student needs to make continual progress, which means each student may need different approaches to learning curriculum.

Prepare for Obstacles

There will be obstacles in the endeavor of collaboration. Here, we summarize some key points that have already been mentioned and key ideas that will be further discussed in later chapters. Overall, these are 10 lessons learned through a qualitative study of implementing collaboration as a service for gifted students (adapted from Mofield, 2020b):

1. **Communicate clear purposes and roles.** Both the gifted education teacher and classroom teacher need to understand the purpose of collaboration and the roles they play in a shared commitment of planning and delivering instruction.

2. **Build relationships and trust.** Remember that collaboration is a complex interpersonal process that must be established on the foundation of trust. Use the TEAM frame (trust, engage, align, maintain) to sustain a supportive working relationship.

3. **Elicit administrative support.** Administrators are key players in making collaboration work. As previously mentioned, they can secure professional learning on collaboration; align master schedules for collaboration; resolve dilemmas with space, time, and allocation of resources; and model participation in PLCs where the needs of students who have already demonstrated mastery of material are discussed. Administrators should work to ensure collaboration is accountable and sustainable (Friend et al., 2010).

4. **Work with the welcoming.** Work with teachers who want to collaborate. You will more likely gain the trust, engagement, alignment, and maintenance of the relationship that collaboration requires. It may be a good idea to start with teachers who are viewed as leaders or influencers within the school. Those who are eager and excited to learn new strategies may be more likely to share about positive collaboration experiences with others.

5. **Build a tool kit.** Provide clear definitions for terms such as *differentiation*, *high-level thinking*, *depth*, and *complexity*. Be equipped with high-quality gifted curriculum and resources and models to share with teachers. Many teachers are eager to learn about them, see them modeled, or talk with

someone about applying them to their classroom context (see Chapters 6–7).

6. **Plan to coplan.** Collaboration cannot work without the time reserved to do it. Common planning time should be built in the schedule, and this can be organized and supported by administrators. Teachers should coplan for at least 30 minutes per week (Landrum, 2001) with set goals for sessions (Kane & Henning, 2004).

7. **Use a framework for differentiation.** Adopt a differentiation or curriculum model that everyone understands and that fits the context of your gifted program. Common language around differentiated practices can help facilitate a culture of collaboration.

8. **Implement differentiation together, not "different" activities.** Collaboration must remain student focused rather than activity driven. It may be tempting for gifted education teachers to share ideas for lessons in which students engage in an activity "different" from a typical lesson, but not really differentiated. Such activities are often popular to students, but lack the rigor needed for continued learning. There must be intentional depth or complexity tied to the content of the lesson (see Chapter 3).

9. **Reflect and revise.** Learning to harmonize in collaboration can take time. Reflecting on the past provides important feedback for the future. All teachers involved in collaborative work should plan for time to consider the following questions: "What impact did this have on student learning (on both the gifted students and other students in the classroom)? How do we know? What are our next steps? How can we support each other in these next steps?"

10. **Continually evaluate the role of collaboration in the context of the gifted program.** To what extent is it meeting the needs of gifted learners? How is collaboration accomplishing the overall goals of the gifted program? How is this affecting student learning?

Changing Practices Is Not Easy

Perhaps collaborative teaching is a new practice for you and other classroom teachers. At the start of any change process, there are inevitable challenges along the way. You may encounter reluctance from teachers who may not want to share instructional space or spend valuable planning time with you. In a recent qualitative study conducted by Mofield (2020b), many classroom teachers were concerned about staying on track with a set scope and sequence. Veering from the prescribed plan by modifying instruction for gifted learners was perceived to be a threat to daily routines. There was also a lack of buy-in in understanding how working with a gifted education teacher would benefit all learners in the classroom or how it would be a valuable investment of their time.

Much of this was due to what we commonly see in change initiatives—the implementation dip. Fullan (2001) described this as "a dip in performance and confidence as one encounters an innovation that requires new skills and new understandings" (p. 6). Knowing that the implementation dip will likely happen can prepare you for moving through the dip. From the perspective of a classroom teacher, collaboration efforts that lead to changes in instructional practices or sharing classroom space involve stepping into the unknown, which can indeed be uncomfortable. When a teacher steps out of their comfort zone to work with you to use new strategies and ideas, this involves vulnerability. This is, again, why it is so important to communicate clear roles, work through the TEAM frame, and have the right tools and know-how for collaboration. This makes the uncharted path a bit more known and visible, deescalating the threat and fear of the unknown.

In order to build impactful, lasting, sustainable change, all involved must have a clear understanding of why collaboration is necessary, and leaders must set the stage for a cultural shift. For collaboration to be a part of the normal day-to-day practices within a school culture, it involves system change, not just a "tinkering" change. A tinkering change is a change that addresses a particular deficit or need, but a system change is a change in the overall structure and mission of the district (Hubbard, 2009). Many times, classroom collaboration is seen as an add-on part of instruction rather than part of the overall structure of the district's goals. Collaboration is likely not to be effective if it relies entirely on the gifted education teacher asking to coplan and coteach with teachers who may not understand the need or purpose of the collaboration. In the qualitative study by Mofield (2020b), classroom teachers perceived a clash in what the district valued (i.e., increasing student performance on state test scores, following a scope and sequence) versus what gifted education teachers valued (i.e., providing differentiation through acceleration and enrichment in the regular classroom).

Collaboration must be viewed and emphasized as valuable by district leadership and communicated as part of the district's overall plan to teach and challenge all learners. Sustainable collaboration requires a transformational cultural shift facilitated by administrators seeking input from teachers and considering their underlying beliefs and values. As emphasized previously, sustaining practice also requires resources and ongoing opportunities for quality professional learning so that teaching partners can grow and sharpen their skills in collaboration efforts.

In any new initiative related to instruction or curriculum, understanding teachers' previous experiences and existing perceptions, attitudes, and beliefs is important in order to make connections with new practices and ideas (Zhao et al., 2002). Although providing professional learning in coteaching and collaboration is a good start, other efforts involving follow-up interactions through peer coaching and ongoing collegial support can provide feedback and opportunity for deep reflection within the collaborative partnership.

Moving Forward

Although there will be obstacles along the way, you can prepare for them. Focus on starting with small wins in collaboration by sharing resources with teachers as an invitation to later "colabor" and "cothink" together in the future. Use this momentum to keep moving forward. Over time, these efforts will pay off as others see the value of collaborative work and its benefits on student learning.

Chapter 3

Basic Principles for Coplanning Differentiated Instruction

This chapter focuses on integrating the expertise of two or more teachers to coplan differentiated instruction. Collaboration through coplanning involves shared decision making, although it may or may not lead to coteaching. There may be times when the gifted education teacher is not able to directly work with students, but during the coplanning process, they can support the classroom teacher through cocreating differentiated resources and enrichment activities to supplement a lesson.

This chapter presents basic principles for coplanning differentiated instruction, including using preassessments, features of differentiation, and methods of assessment. Further, we provide a framework to share with teachers for guiding students through independent study. We emphasize that the sharing of strategies proposed throughout this chapter should involve shared decision making, not just a one-way offering of suggested ideas to use.

Know Thy Student

Teachers must "know thy student." Considering the student's interest and readiness level through preassessment is the starting point for differentiation.

Preassessment does not have to be a difficult, complicated endeavor. Teachers can use end-of-unit posttests as preassessments to determine how much of the content students already know. Short assessments asking students to explain what they know about certain concepts can show insight regarding a student's understanding of the material before it is taught. For example, concept maps can help teachers understand how students perceive relationships between ideas. A teacher may ask students to make a concept map to show what they know about biomes before teaching a unit on them. Through concept mapping, students demonstrate their understanding of how ideas and terms about the topic connect to each other.

Assessing student readiness better informs instructional practice, streamlines units of study for differentiation, and measures student growth over time. From here, both teachers can coplan how flexible groups might be formed. For students who have already shown mastery of material, they can move forward in their learning to have opportunities to learn more advanced content. Known as curriculum compacting, the content they know can be replaced with accelerated content or enrichment (Renzulli & Reis, 2014).

During coplanning, the classroom teacher may share the overall instructional goals for the unit, while the gifted education teacher can offer advanced instructional strategies to support how gifted learners interact with the content (including acceleration, adding depth and complexity, etc.). Note that flexible groups should be used throughout a unit of study. Results from preassessments should inform how students are grouped for differentiation, not labels of "gifted" or "not gifted."

Preassessments also provide a greater depth of insight when examining summative data to determine overall content mastery and student growth. Consider the following scenario: Upon grading an end-of-unit assessment, Student A scored 100% and Student B scored 74%. Based on these data, Student B did not demonstrate the same level of content mastery as Student A. These results are surprising, as Student A exhibited multiple behavior problems and regularly showed inattention throughout the unit, while Student B was consistently focused and putting forth effort. If preassessment data were available signifying that Student A scored 98% and Student B scored 12% at the onset of the unit, then this information provides a greater understanding of the growth of learning from each student. In this case, Student B demonstrated significant growth, and Student A had little opportunity to progress at all. This also explains Student A's behavior and inattention related to lack of challenge and new learning.

Learning Environments That Promote Success

Consider the question, "What contexts promote achievement for gifted learners, and which contexts stifle achievement?" All students need motivating learning environments that promote engagement. When thinking specifically about the gifted learner, you must consider how characteristics of giftedness impact achievement motivation.

Some gifted students have not had challenging learning experiences early in their schooling. They have become accustomed to doing well on easy work. When presented with work that requires effort, they may feel quite uncomfortable, perceiving the challenge as a threat to their "smart" sense of self. If students are provided challenging curriculum early on and throughout their school experiences, it prevents them from developing risk avoidance in later school experiences. Unfortunately, many gifted students never have opportunities to develop important self-regulation skills or positive achievement attitudes (e.g., growth mindset, perseverance). Thus, challenging curriculum provides the soil for self-regulation skills to grow. We say this to emphasize the importance of teaching each child in their zone of proximal development (Vygotsky, 1978), where they feel stretched just beyond their comfort zones.

Siegle and McCoach (2005) described key components that promote achievement in gifted learners within their Achievement Orientation Model. This includes (1) self-efficacy, the belief that one has the skills to accomplish a task; (2) goal-valuation, the belief that the goal or task is a worthy pursuit because it is meaningful to the learner; and (3) environmental perception, the belief that "I can be successful here" because of the perceived support from the context. These three factors work together to ignite self-regulation, the ability to manage oneself to work toward meeting goals. Therefore, in creating contexts for a conducive learning environment, these factors can be considered and deliberately cultivated in the classroom climate.

Differentiation

The word *differentiation* is often used in education, but difficult to put into practice. VanTassel-Baska (2015) defined the process of differentiation as "the deliberate adaptation and modification of the curriculum, instructional processes, and assessments to respond to the needs of gifted learners" (p. 81). Differentiation is not a bag of tricks used to plug into low-quality curriculum; rather, it is a philosophy rooted in effective teaching (Doubet & Hockett, 2015). Unfortunately, some teachers see differentiation as simply providing choice to students for various types of projects to do rather than a deliberate response to students' needs. True, providing choices may appeal to various student interests, but to challenge and stimulate the gifted learner, the instructional plan should include differentiating the rigor of the task. This is explained through the following quadrants of vertical and horizontal differentiation in Figure 3.

Quadrant III illustrates instruction or tasks that are boring and bland, like Corn Flakes cereal. There is a low level of rigor and low level of student interest in the task. The task could be modified with some "added sugar and marshmallows," like Lucky Charms cereal, to be more appealing to the learner, moving the task into Quadrant IV (Fluff and Stuff), but the task still lacks rigor. For example, students may enjoy being given a choice to make a puppet, design a diorama, or develop a fancy Prezi presentation, but without expectations for additional depth, complexity, or critical thinking, the task completion will not lead to deep learning. This is a type of horizontal differentiation. It is more appealing to the learner but does not provide adequate challenge. By contrast, Quadrant II involves compliant learning. This is when the learner is engaged with challenging curriculum, but the tasks are not engaging or tied to student interests. There is adequate rigor, but not adequate relevance. This type of sugar-free "Shredded Wheat" may help the learner stretch and grow, but it is overall boring and bland. Then, Quadrant I shows the authentic learning zone where the learner engages with more in-depth learning of the rigorous content tied to their interests and value systems. This is represented by the wholesome goodness of a full breakfast packed with protein (scrambled eggs and bacon), whole grain toast, and a side of fruit. This type of hearty learning sticks with the learner; it's meaningful, relevant, and rigorous, nourishing the learner's growth.

The ABCs of Planning for Gifted Learners

So, how do you provide the authentic type of learning when coplanning with gifted students in mind? We provide the ABCs: advance the content, build the buy-in, and create challenge (Mofield, 2019). This is based on the rationale that gifted students are able to work through content more quickly and can think about complex, abstract ideas. Based on best practices in gifted education, the ABCs shown in Table 7 can provide a structure for thinking about how to codesign instruction for gifted learners.

FIGURE 3
Vertical and Horizontal Differentiation

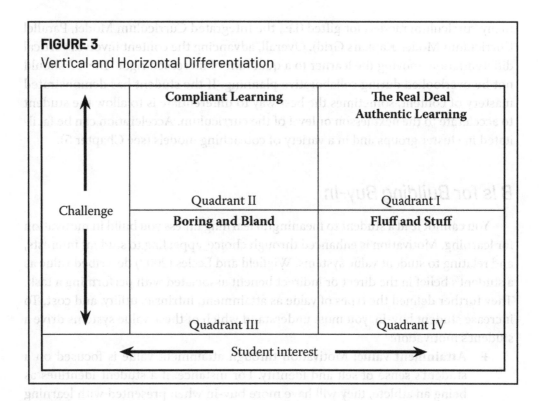

TABLE 7
The ABCs of Differentiation

Advance the Content	Build Buy-In	Create Challenge
+ Accelerate the content and pace	+ Build in choices	+ Open inquiry
+ Provide advanced resources	+ Harness motivation	+ Depth/complexity
+ Introduce advanced vocabulary/concepts	+ Create task value:	+ Critical thinking
	○ Tied to identity	+ Creative thinking
	○ Tied to interest	+ High-level thinking
+ Content-expert thinking	○ Tied to future	+ Abstract thinking
	○ Worth time and effort	+ Posing boundaries

Note. From *Curriculum, Planning, and Instruction for Gifted Learners* [Conference session], by E. Mofield, 2019, Kentucky Association for the Gifted Conference, Lexington, KY, United States. Reprinted with permission of the author.

A Is for Advance the Content

This includes accelerating the pace of instruction, providing higher level vocabulary, providing more advanced resources, using above-grade-level content, or combining multiple standards. Advancing the content is a differentiation feature in many curriculum models for gifted (i.e., the Integrated Curriculum Model, Parallel Curriculum Model, Kaplan's Grid). Overall, advancing the content involves vertical differentiation, moving the learner to a quadrant of increased rigor. The "A" should not be overlooked during collaborative planning. If the student has demonstrated mastery of content, sometimes the best way to differentiate is to allow the student to accelerate to the next lesson or level of the curriculum. Acceleration can be facilitated in cluster groups and in a variety of coteaching models (see Chapter 5).

B Is for Building Buy-In

You cannot lead a student to meaningful learning unless you build in motivation for learning. Motivation is enhanced through choice, appealing to student interests, and relating to student value systems. Wigfield and Eccles (2002) described value as a student's belief in the direct or indirect benefit associated with performing a task. They further defined the types of value as attainment, intrinsic, utility, and cost. To increase student buy-in, you must understand which of these value systems drive a student's motivation:

+ **Attainment value:** Motivation through attainment value is focused on a student's sense of self and identity. For instance, if a student identifies as being an athlete, they will have more buy-in when presented with learning experiences related to health, physical activity, or sports; likewise, if a student identifies as a scholar, they will be more motivated engaging in rigorous academic discourse.

+ **Intrinsic value:** When working to increase student buy-in through intrinsic value, the learning task needs to be closely aligned with a student's interests. For example, if a student is highly interested in the arts, activities focused on design, art critique, or working with different mediums (e.g., art supplies) would increase buy-in.

+ **Utility value:** Students who are driven by this value system are motivated by recognizing how their current learning will benefit them in their future. This is quite often the case for students who enroll in Advanced Placement (AP) courses, as they value the opportunity to earn college credit while still in high school. They see this as an advantage in the college acceptance process and, ultimately, obtaining a career in their desired areas of study.

+ **Cost:** In contrast to the previous types of value, cost focuses on the perceived sacrifice a student must make to engage in a task. Consider a student who has a homework assignment to complete. If the student would rather be watching TV, engaging in social media, or hanging with friends instead of completing the assignment, the cost, or sacrifice, is too large. In this case, the teacher needs to evaluate how to increase the value of the assignment to overcome the student's perceived sacrifice.

C Is for Creating Challenge

Creating challenge includes embedding differentiation features that bring students into their zone of proximal development where they are stretched in their learning. We will discuss a number of specific strategies in Chapters 6 and 7 that can elevate the level of challenge for instruction. This includes developing opportunities for open inquiry; adding depth and complexity to tasks; intentionally building in critical thinking, creative thinking, higher level thinking, and abstract thinking; and posing parameters on tasks.

During the collaborative process, the ABCs can be applied when considering what to do for a student who has demonstrated mastery of content. For example, if a student has already demonstrated an understanding of the key facts and details about Ancient Egypt, the student's interest in mummification could be utilized in an assignment that allows for additional exploration of the topic as it reflects the importance of Ancient Egyptian culture. The student could be provided with advanced materials and resources on the topic to complete an independent study (see I-LEARN in this chapter). Beyond finding and reporting facts, the student might make thematic connections (abstract thinking) to the overarching big ideas of stability and change, answering the questions, "How does mummification allow for stability? Does mummification allow for any change?" Additional complexity could be added by studying mummification practices from ethical, cultural, and societal perspectives of the time.

The ABCs also offer a variety of differentiation features to consider when coplanning. For example, you may be working with a teacher to coplan a lesson related to real-world issues in environmental science, such as the decline of the honeybee population. During the coplanning process, both teachers may consider the A (advance the content) by selecting advanced resources, including exposure to above-grade-level resources on the topic, and providing excerpts from scientific journals. Working both from B (building buy-in) and C (creating challenge), both teachers might work to develop 2–4 student product choices related to the content. The choices from a variety of challenging tasks can create and enhance motivation. Table 8 provides a variety of ways that challenge can be enhanced while students study honeybee decline. In addition, Chapters 6 and 7 provide additional ways to coplan instruction through the use of specific strategies and overall approaches to instructional design. Within the features, many aspects indeed overlap. For example, within open inquiry, students apply critical thinking, complexity, and creative thinking.

TABLE 8
Features of "Creating Challenge"

	Meaning	Example Application
Open Inquiry	Develop tasks with few parameters where students explore issues or problems.	Implement problem-based learning about the issue of the honeybee population decreasing. Students examine and define the problem and develop multiple solutions.
Depth	Examine issues, trends, details, and patterns of a discipline (Kaplan, 2009).	Pose a problem or issue (e.g., Should farmers continue to use pesticides to increase food yield?). Students analyze details, trends, tools of the discipline, and patterns related to answering the question.
Complexity	Make connections among multiple ideas, observe relationships between concepts, and understand multiple perspectives (Kaplan, 2009; VanTassel-Baska & Stambaugh, 2006).	Ask students to examine how the decreased bee population is the result of multiple factors and how it affects social, economic, and cultural systems.
Critical Thinking	Use reason and logic to analyze, evaluate, and construct arguments.	Students critically analyze the pros, cons, biased perspectives, and effects of using pesticides and/or genetically modified crops.
Creative Thinking	Look at problems with new perspectives with an aim to create something new.	Students develop multiple creative solutions for increasing the honeybee population and elaborate in detail how an original solution addresses the issue.
High-Level Thinking	Analyze, evaluate, or synthesize information (from Bloom's taxonomy).	Students analyze multiple causes and effects of the bee population decreasing, evaluating effects on various points of view (farmers, environmentalists, consumers), and create an idea for an innovative form of technology to address the issue.

TABLE 8, *continued*

	Meaning	Example Application
Abstract Thinking	Link content to themes and big ideas (e.g., conflict, cycles, patterns, interactions, systems; VanTasssel-Baska & Stambaugh, 2006). Apply principles and theories. Create metaphors and symbols.	Apply a concept such as patterns by asking, "How does the decrease in the bee population affect patterns within other systems (agricultural, economic, other species, etc.)?"
Posing Boundaries	Make a task more challenging by posing set criteria and constraints within the task (Stambaugh, 2018).	Develop a proposal that includes ways for farmers to decrease the use of pesticides while also increasing food yield.

Tiered Differentiation

Tiering is a popular differentiation technique that involves the process of determining which students need more support, which students are performing at grade level, and which students need opportunities for deeper or extended learning. Preassessments and ongoing formative assessments provide the needed information to gauge these readiness levels, which are key factors in successful tiering. In addition, flexible grouping options should be discussed as part of coplanning, as students' readiness levels might fluctuate depending on background knowledge, the rate at which information is learned, and students' sustained interest in the subject. Once student readiness levels are identified, coplanning focuses on creating different tiers, or levels, of activities that best meet students' learning needs.

When creating tiered assignments, collaboration should address content standards. Identify what content and skills need to be mastered and plan accordingly. For gifted learners, the gifted education teacher would work closely with the classroom teacher to plan for the highest tier of learning by sharing strategies to increase depth, complexity, and critical thinking applied to advanced content. During coplanning, the teachers might incorporate features from other strategies in this chapter or additional strategies from Chapter 6 for vertical differentiation.

Invisible Tiering

Another consideration when coplanning for tiered differentiation is what we refer to as invisible tiering. Invisible tiering does not change how the content is differentiated, but it does affect how students are presented with the varied learning tasks. Whenever possible, create a learning environment in which the tiered activities are not outwardly evident to the students. For example, if the classroom teacher and gifted education teacher coplan a lesson on using the order of operations to solve equations, the two teachers would brainstorm creative ways to "mask" the different levels needed for tiered differentiation. In this case, teachers might place differing levels of equations into various colored plastic eggs. The classroom teacher would instruct students to locate only certain colored eggs around the room. Not only would this help to ensure that all students have an opportunity to find the hidden eggs, but also each color would represent a different learning tier. As an additional idea, different leveled questions, reading selections, equations, etc., could be integrated into QR codes on different colored papers placed around the room. Students would be assigned a color, based on readiness levels, and they would scan the codes around the classroom as they worked their way through the designated assignment. Using invisible tiering is all about being creative in coplanning and engaging students in their learning, so they are not focused on who is working on which level.

Self-Selected Graduated Difficulty

Self-selected graduated difficulty involves students self-selecting a tiered learning assignment based on their own present levels of understanding. This is done by creating an environment built on clear expectations and trust. The appropriate tier is self-selected only after each student takes the opportunity to analyze and articulate the knowledge needed to successfully complete each level. Once this is accomplished, each student chooses the most appropriate level to meet their needs, while also being allowed the flexibility to work up or down as needed. If students need additional challenge beyond the highest tier, they are directed to create the next higher level in the tiered assignment and explain how it is more challenging. Students work to complete and evaluate their chosen level of work, reflect on goals for improvement, and articulate how to continue toward a higher goal. Although lessons are most commonly tiered by content, they may also be tiered through the thinking process involved or the type of product required to demonstrate mastery. After the gifted education teacher and classroom teacher create the tiered activities, students work through the self-selected graduated difficulty as they learn to:

1. analyze each tier and articulate the knowledge needed to successfully complete each task (e.g., students should be able to answer the following ques-

TABLE 9
Sample Graduated Difficulty Tiered Assignments

Math Tiers: Solving Equations With Variables	Language Arts Tiers: Poetry Analysis
+ **Level 1:** Simple equation, solving with two or less operations for one variable with positive integers + **Level 2:** Solving for one variable, including three to four operations and with positive and negative integers + **Level 3:** Similar to Level 2, but including two equations to solve for two variables	In order of increasingly complex interpretation: + **Level 1:** "Sonnet 18" by William Shakespeare with accompanying analysis activity examining structure and style + **Level 2:** "A Little Learning Is a Dangerous Thing" by Alexander Pope with accompanying analysis activity comparing the theme to another text + **Level 3:** "3 Stances" by William Carlos Williams with accompanying analysis activity defending the symbolism of each character as it relates to the historical context of the poem

tions: What makes one level harder than the next? What skills or knowledge would be needed to complete each task? What level do you think would work best for you? Why?);

2. self-select the appropriate tier based on individual readiness levels;
3. complete the task and/or recognize if a different level is better suited for independent practice;
4. assess work from provided answer keys; and
5. reflect through metacognitive analysis of work and set new goals.

Table 9 provides sample graduated difficulty tiered activities for math and language arts.

Bumping Up Bloom's

Most teachers are familiar with Bloom's (1956) taxonomy. Teachers are encouraged to incorporate high-level thinking for all learners in the classroom, especially at the analyze, evaluate, and create levels. The upper levels of Bloom's taxonomy can be further enhanced with additional features of abstractness, critical thinking, complexity, and context (for transfer of knowledge). Resource 2: Bumping Up Bloom's Taxonomy shows examples of how questions can be tiered with additional features that extend students' thinking.

Assessment

Assessment helps answer the question, "To what extent do students know and understand the content?" When providing opportunities for gifted students to show what they know through differentiated tasks, you should also have a plan for differentiating assessments. When coplanning a lesson, both the gifted education teacher and classroom teacher might consider the role of rubrics and grading criteria for such tasks. For example, while working with a classroom teacher, the gifted education teacher may use the teacher-created rubric but offer ways to modify it that extend the ceiling for gifted students to demonstrate their learning.

The differentiated rubric might also reflect many of the differentiation features highlighted in Table 10. Beyond completion and appearance criteria, rubrics may specifically include ways to measure how the learning reflects the application, advanced content, critical thinking, creative thinking, and/or high-level thinking relevant to content. These rubrics are also useful for self-assessments and reflection on students' own personal learning and growth. Table 10 includes an example of a rubric that highlights such features.

In addition, Roberts and Inman's (2015) Developing and Assessing Product (DAP) Tool is a way to guide both the development and assessment of differentiated products. These tools provide three rubrics of increasing sophistication (Tier 1, Tier 2, and Tier 3) for a variety of product types, including posters, presentations, models, websites, and more. The components are based on content, creativity, presentation, and reflection using standards of criteria ranging from 0–6 (nonparticipating, nonperforming, novice, progressing, proficient, advanced, and professional). The levels of assessment provide criteria that remove ceilings for students. For example, to achieve a "professional" score of a 6, the student must demonstrate what is expected of a professional in the content area, exceeding even advanced expectations of meeting a standard (see Chapter 11 for facilitating mentorships with professionals). Beyond serving as an excellent differentiated assessment tool for teachers, when students are shown the DAP rubrics ahead of time, they have a clear understanding of criteria for developing their products and focusing their learning (Roberts & Inman, 2015).

	Analyze	Evaluate	Create
Typical Example Stems	+ What are the parts? + How do they relate?	+ Which is better, ____ or ____ ? + How would you decide ____ ?	+ Create your own ____ . + Develop a solution to ____ .
Added Abstractness + Big Idea + Metaphors + Symbols + Themes + Generalizations + Theories	Create a metaphor for ____ , and explain how the metaphor demonstrates how the parts of ____ work together.	+ Is the generalization always applicable? Why or why not? + What criteria do we need to understand if this theory/generalization is true?	+ Create your own version of ____ to reflect the big idea. + Create a symbol to convey the big idea/theme.
Added Critical Thinking + Implications + Effects/Results + Assumptions + Point of View + Bias	What part is least necessary to the system? What would be the long-term result if it were missing?	What assumptions are involved in deciding which is better? What perspectives should we consider?	Create your own version to show a different perspective, including assumptions associated with that perspective. What are the implications of thinking about it differently?
Added Complexity More variables, relationships, interactions	How do the parts establish cause-effect relationships? Examine ____ through multiple perspectives and themes.	What criteria would you develop to determine the best ____ ? How might others view this criteria? How does this criteria relate to your overall goal?	Create your own version to show how ____ affects ____ .
Added Context	How might this system of parts/interactions apply to other settings?	Can you think of situations in which ____ would be better?	Create your own version of ____ that would fit the context of ____ .

Note. Adapted from "What Makes Honors Classes More Than a Name?", by E. Mofield, in press, *AMLE Magazine*.

TABLE 10
Example Rubric With Differentiation Features

	4 Exceeds Expectations	3 Meets Expectations	2 Approaches Expectations and Needs Effort	1 Needs Effort
Content	Demonstrates application of advanced vocabulary, language of the discipline, and accurate portrayal of newly learned content. Makes insightful connections to other content within and outside the discipline. Student supplies additional criteria:	Demonstrates application of grade-level vocabulary, language of the discipline, and accurate portrayal of newly learned content. Makes some connections to content within and outside the discipline.	Demonstrates some application of grade-level vocabulary, language of the discipline, and portrayal of newly learned content, although some elements may be missing. Only loose connections are made to content within or outside the discipline.	Does not demonstrate adequate application of grade-level vocabulary, language of the discipline, and portrayal of newly learned content. Little or no connections are made to content within or outside the discipline.
Creative Thinking	Shows substantive evidence of many, varied, elaborate, and/or original ideas applied to the content.	Shows some evidence of many, varied, elaborate, and/or original ideas applied to content.	Shows little evidence of many, varied, elaborate, and/or original thinking applied to content.	Does not show evidence of creative thinking. Demonstrates only summary of facts.
Critical Thinking	Demonstrates logical reasoning through perspective-taking, use of evidence, and analysis of implications. Applies the thinking process of an expert in the field (thinking as a historian, etc.).	Demonstrates some logical reasoning through perspective-taking, use of evidence, and analysis of implications. Applies the thinking process of an expert in the field (thinking as a historian, etc.).	Demonstrates some reasoning, although there might be gaps in connections and logical explanations. Use of perspective-taking, use of evidence, and analysis of implications can be improved.	Little or no evidence of logical reasoning throughout the product.
Product	High-quality product is reflective of what an expert might produce in the field or discipline.	High-quality product demonstrates learning related to the content area.	Product demonstrates learning related to the content area.	Product lacks detail and/or does not adequately reflect content learning.

Coplanning for Independent Study

Although multiple strategies are effective with gifted learners within the regular education classroom, there are times when a classroom teacher needs to differentiate for the needs of one student. In this situation, working collaboratively to design an independent unit of study is a viable course of action. Preassessments, as discussed earlier in this chapter, are essential components to this process. (We should also note, beyond meeting the needs of just one student, independent study may also be a part of a larger coplanning endeavor for many or all students in the classroom.)

Quite often, information collected from these preassessments leads to flexible grouping, tiered lessons, and compacting of curricula for students who demonstrate mastery of concepts at the onset of a unit of study. What happens, however, when there is only one student in a classroom of 30 who demonstrates this level of mastery? How will the extra time be spent if lessons are compacted for this student? Unfortunately, in noncollaborative environments, this often leads to the gifted student becoming a teacher's assistant within the classroom or a peer tutor, both of which lead to underachievement and frustration for the gifted learner.

To address this issue, independent study can guide gifted learners deeper into specific classroom content or provide an opportunity to explore an area of interest. This decision should be based on the purpose or desired learning outcome and discussed as part of the collaborative process. In any case, it is strongly recommended that the gifted student be involved in developing the independent study, as this has been found to increase both the critical thinking and motivation of the gifted learner (Powers, 2008).

By continuing to work through the ABCs of planning for gifted learners, an independent study focuses on differentiating through content, process, and/or product and should be structured in a manner conducive to student success. The I-LEARN Process (Identify a Topic to Investigate, Lay out a Learning Plan, Engage in Research, Apply Learning, Reflect and Refine, and Next Steps for Newfound Knowledge; Phelps, in press) provides a structure for collaboratively creating a successful independent study unit and ensures student learning to be relevant, rigorous, and reflective (see Table 11). As with any instructional strategy, the design process should take into consideration the specific needs of the individual student (e.g., student age, academic needs, affective needs, student strengths, etc.).

Through collaborative efforts in coplanning, you might encourage research approaches authentic to the discipline (e.g., "How might a historian/scientist/literary scholar think about the research question?" or "If you could ask an expert any question about your topic, what would you ask?"). Students also have an opportunity to develop important psychosocial skills, including working toward a

TABLE 11
I-LEARN Steps to Creating Successful Independent Study

	I-LEARN Steps	To-Do List
I	Identify a Topic to Investigate	1. Determine if the independent study should focus on a deeper, more complex examination of preassessment content (e.g., thinking as a disciplinarian to solve a related world issue with applied skills), or should the independent study be based on student interest? 2. Include the student in the I-LEARN Process as appropriate. 3. Decide if the independent study will be approached through description, cause/effect, comparison, or problem/solution. 4. Determine the form of research the independent study will take (e.g., case study, explanatory, historical, correlation, experimental, action, etc.).
L	Lay Out a Learning Plan	1. Create an Independent Learning Contract to be signed by the student, teacher, and parent. 2. Create a list of learning components with accompanying rubrics. When selecting these tasks, provide the student with options and outline what is expected for successful completion of each task. 3. Establish what materials (e.g., notebook, graphic organizers, reflection sheets, sources, handouts, etc.) are needed and where they will be stored. 4. Determine what types of resources will be utilized to accomplish the I-LEARN goals (e.g., books, videos, interviews, computer, poster board, etc.). 5. Construct a timeline for completion dates along with preestablished check-in dates.
E	Engage in Research	1. Create guiding research question(s). 2. Establish how the research will be organized and maintained. 3. Determine how sources will be cited.
A	Apply Learning	1. Create an authentic culminating task for synthesis of learned information with an accompanying rubric. 2. Identify real-world connection/application.

TABLE 11, *continued*

	I-LEARN Steps	To-Do List
R	Reflect and Refine	1. Determine how student reflection will be part of the independent study process. 2. Create specific questions to guide the student in the reflective/refinement process of learning (e.g., *What did I do well? What would I do differently?*). 3. Specify how the teacher will provide additional feedback during the scheduled check-ins.
N	Next Steps for Newfound Knowledge	1. Determine how the components of learning will be shared with an identified audience. 2. Identify potential next steps for future research.

Note. Adapted from "Differentiation Through Independent Study: The I-LEARN Process," by V. Phelps, in A. Quinzio-Zafran and E. Wilkins (Eds.), *The New Teacher's Guide to Overcoming Common Challenges: Curated Advice From Award Winning Teachers*, in press, Routledge.

long-term goal, establishing timelines for progress, and reflecting on overcoming challenges throughout the process. Overall, this is an opportunity to cultivate student strengths and allow them to explore interests in academic domains.

The I-LEARN Process is applicable across any content area and grade level. For example, when speaking with a second-grade student who has already demonstrated mastery for unit of study, the teacher realizes the student has a great deal of interest in the human body and its various systems. Using the I-LEARN Process, the teacher and student together decide that the independent study will focus on an explanatory, comparative study on the digestive, circulatory, and respiratory systems of the human body. Learning tasks involve reading various texts with a specific focus on determining importance and participating in several online dissections and scientific interactions. A learning contract and timeline for completion are established. Throughout the independent study, the student seeks out answers to the guiding question ("How do the digestive, circulatory, and respiratory systems work together as subsystems to contribute to the human body system?"). As the synthesis task, the student creates a physical model of the human body that includes interactive elements, signifying how the various subsystems contribute to one another and to the whole human body. The student chooses to share the information in a presentation using the model to support an argument for how the system would be impacted by a blood clot. For future research possibilities, the student poses, "How do blood diseases affect these systems?" Student reflection and consistent and constructive feedback is provided throughout the independent study process. The teacher might consider using the DAP Tool (Roberts & Inman, 2015) mentioned earlier in this chapter to assess the student's product.

Collaborative Decision Making

This chapter included an overview of the basic process for coplanning differentiated instruction, specifically for gifted students. Depending on the context, the coplanning may serve to support the classroom teacher in differentiating instruction or lead to coteaching a lesson together (see Chapter 5). In the spirit of collaboration, coplanning integrates the expertise of each party, involves shared decision making, and allows for active learning. Now that you know the "what" of coplanning for differentiation, the "how" follows in the next chapter.

Chapter 4

Coplanning in Practice

How does knowing about the principles of coplanning for differentiation instruction translate into actually coplanning? This chapter provides practical tips for coplanning lesson plans and long-term units, including opportunities to do so in creative space and professional learning communities. This chapter also presents modeling (sometimes called demonstration teaching) as a way to share strategies that can be used in the future by a classroom teacher. Transfer of knowledge occurs when coplanning and/or modeling is followed by reflecting on how students responded to the lesson, why specific strategies were used, and how the strategies might be used in future lessons.

Coplanning Within the Collaborative Process Model

Thinking back to the Collaborative Process Model (see Figure 1, p. 14), coplanning should begin with a purpose and goal for collaboration (e.g., to develop a preassessment, to develop a tiered assignment to use with a set of standards, to determine which students need compacting, to plan a coteaching lesson, etc.). Then, during the planning stage, both teachers determine specifically what needs to be done and by whom. Such deliberate planning can help make the collaborative process more productive and efficient, while making differentiation easier and more manageable, given that there is a shared responsibility for student learning.

As emphasized in the previous chapters, the collaboration process should be situated within the TEAM frame (trust, engage, align, and maintain). Intentional efforts must be made to establish a positive collaborative partnership. Here, we offer tips on applying TEAM to coplanning:

+ **T—Trust:** Follow through on tasks that you say you will do. Trust the expertise the other teacher offers in the partnership. Presume positive intent through all interactions.
+ **E—Engage:** Engage each other by sincerely listening to one another and asking questions. Try to refrain from one person being the leader in the collaborative relationship. Endeavor to seek out the valuable expertise in each other and provide praise and encouragement for the ideas exchanged through this shared commitment.
+ **A—Align:** Openly discuss how comfortable the classroom teacher is in using various differentiated approaches. Teachers have different tolerance for noise and student freedom in the classroom. If you are working with a classroom teacher who primarily relies on traditional approaches, have discussions on how differentiation features may or may not align with this teaching style and what can be done to align beliefs and practices.
+ **M—Maintain:** Maintenance can bring accountability to the relationship. The positive relationship is maintained only when there is open dialogue about the functionality of the collaborative relationship. Remove the fear of giving each other feedback by inviting feedback from each other. During maintenance, both teachers should feel they can openly critique the coplanning and coteaching process and offer suggestions for future implementation (Landrum, 2002).

Before coplanning lessons with a classroom teacher, visit the teacher's classroom to understand the climate of the classroom, the teacher's instructional style, and student dynamics. This can help set the stage for shared understanding about the goal of the coplanning process—enhancing the learning of all students.

Efficient Coplanning

One of the most difficult parts of coplanning is finding the time to do so. To make coplanning an efficient process that does not compromise the shared decision making of true collaboration, consider ways to prepare ideas and materials before and after a collaborative meeting. As indicated in Table 12, the gifted education teacher may come to the meeting prepared with ideas after already viewing the lesson plan. After the meeting, the classroom teacher and gifted education teacher may have certain responsibilities in preparing activities, assignments, or assessments. Resource 3: Questions, Roles, and Tasks for Coplanning Template serves as a template for asking questions and determining teacher roles in preparation for instruction. If coplanning leads to coteaching, partners may need to coplan more details of the actual implementation of the lesson, which is discussed in Chapter 5.

Long-Term Planning

As teachers develop a collaborative relationship over time as "thinking partners," both might consider how to plan for meeting broader learning goals beyond the content standards. To do this, the classroom teacher might share the long-term curriculum scope and sequence plan for meeting content standards, while the gifted education teacher considers how the plan can be aligned with the gifted program's goals or individualized student plans. Although gifted programs vary by design and philosophy, many emphasize the development of critical and creative thinking skills and the use of problem solving applied to advanced content. From our experience, we used the district's Sequence of Skills (see Resource 4) as a resource for planning lessons that build and enhance specific process skills over time in grades K–8. These skills are written using a variety of thinking models (e.g., Kaplan's [2009] tools for thinking, Paul and Elder's [2019] elements of reasoning; see Chapter 6) indicating graduated levels of sophistication in how these thinking models might apply to advanced content. A resource like this can be useful for both the gifted education teacher and classroom teacher as they brainstorm ways content standards and advanced processing of the content overlap. Many gifted programs have a scope and sequence that details specific goals and objectives for student learning and can be shared with classroom teachers to facilitate and plan for differentiation.

Modeling

Beyond sharing strategies with the classroom teacher during coplanning to increase the challenge level during instruction, the gifted education teacher can model strategies for classroom teachers to see the strategy in practice. Sometimes called demonstration teaching, modeling allows classroom teachers to observe a gifted education teacher ask questions for critical, creative, and abstract thinking in a classroom context. This can provide clarity on how these instructional approaches specifically meet the needs of gifted students. Seeing the strategies in action also helps the classroom teacher understand how the learning environment might be

TABLE 12
Questions, Roles, and Tasks for Coplanning

Coplanning Questions	Before Meeting	During Meeting	After Meeting
What are the lesson goals and objectives?	Classroom teacher shares lesson plan electronically before the meeting.		
How might we preassess students? How will this impact grouping?	Upon receiving the lesson plan before the meeting, the gifted education teacher considers a variety of materials and differentiation strategies (see Chapters 6–7) and prepares a few ideas to share during the meeting.	Plans for preassessment and groupings are discussed and decided upon together during the meeting.	Classroom teacher prepares preassessment and gives preassessment to students.
What differentiation strategies will we use to advance the content, build the buy-in, and create challenge?		Both teachers decide which strategies will be used and how lesson materials will be prepared.	The gifted education teacher prepares differentiated materials to be used.
How will we assess student learning?	Both teachers have initial ideas based on lesson plan.	Assessment methods are selected together during the meeting. Teachers decide who will create assessments/rubrics.	Rubrics are created or modified.
What are the next steps in student learning?	After the lesson is taught, both teachers review assessments and reflect on the lesson's impact on student learning.	In a follow-up meeting after the lesson, both teachers discuss how differentiation might apply in future lessons.	Both teachers continue to reflect and implement next steps for students to progress in their learning.

Questions, Roles, and Tasks for Coplanning Template

Coplanning Questions	Before Meeting	During Meeting	After Meeting
What are the lesson goals and objectives?			
How might we preassess students? How will this impact grouping?			
What differentiation strategies will we use to advance the content, build the buy-in, and create challenge?			
How will we assess student learning?			
What are the next steps in student learning?			

Gifted Education Guide: Sequence of Skills Applied to Advanced Content

Grades	K-1	2-3	4-5	6	7	8
Advanced Content	Exposure to content domains	Exposure to content domains	Exposure to content domains and problem solving	Exposure to content domains and problem solving	Competency in content domains and problem solving	Competency in content domains and problem solving within a field
	When studying advanced content and/or issue in depth, students will					
Multiple Points of View	Identify how multiple perspectives see the problem differently.	Identify various stakeholder points of view on a given problem.	Examine how a stakeholder can have both positive and negative viewpoints on a given situation.	Examine positive/negative and short-term and long-term implications of multiple perspectives of an issue. Introduce assumptions.	Examine the assumptions behind multiple perspectives of an issue.	Examine the assumptions behind multiple perspectives of an issue, noting how assumptions lead to problems.
Structure/Rules	Analyze how a topic is organized (structure), noting subtopics and rules related to the topic.	Analyze how a topic is organized (structure), noting its rules for order and stability.	Analyze how a topic is organized (structure), noting its rules for order, hierarchies, and relationships between important parts.	Analyze a topic's rules for order, hierarchies, and relationship between parts. Students explore how structure promotes function or malfunction.	Analyze how a problem results from the malfunction of a part of the structure. Students analyze the cause-effect interactions of a structure.	Analyze how structures can be modified to produce function within a system (i.e., apply structure to problem solving).

RESOURCE 4, *continued*

Grades	K-1	2-3	4-5	6	7	8
Unanswered Questions / **Details** / **Language of the Discipline**	Determine unanswered questions, and identify details and language of the discipline.	Determine and explore unanswered questions, identifying and classifying details, noting the language of the discipline.	Determine and explore unanswered questions, identifying and classifying details in hierarchies or comparisons, noting the language of the discipline.	From the point of view of a content expert, determine and explore unanswered questions in the field, classify details for inductive generalizations, and apply language of the discipline within authentic products.	From the point of view of a content expert, determine and explore unanswered questions in the field, classify details for inductive generalizations, and apply language of the discipline within authentic products.	From the point of view of a content expert, explain how unanswered questions have changed over time. Classify details in hierarchies, noting relationships of the details. Apply language of the discipline in authentic products.
Trends / **Patterns**	Analyze how patterns allow for prediction and examine factors that impact trends.	Analyze how patterns help establish inferences about cause-effect relationships. Examine multiple factors that impact trends.	Make predictions from patterns, and analyzing multiple cross-discipline factors that impact trends.	Analyze how patterns help content experts identify problems. Use patterns to identify the underlying problem affecting the trend.	Analyze how patterns help content experts identify problems and predict the impact of problems. Use patterns to identify the underlying problem affecting the trend.	Analyze how patterns help content experts analyze the multiple causes of problems and predict the impact of problems. Use patterns to identify the underlying problem affecting the trend.

Grades	K-1	2-3	4-5	6	7	8
Problems **Controversy** **Change Over Time** **Multiple Disciplines**	Analyze how a problem has changed over time.	Analyze how a problem has changed over time and affects multiple disciplines.	Analyze how a problem has changed over time and what it might be like in the future (by analyzing trends and patterns). Continue to analyze effects on multiple disciplines.	Analyze how a problem has changed over time and what it might be like in the future, noting its origin and how factors converged to cause the problem.	Analyze how a problem has changed over time and what it might be like in the future, noting its origin and how factors converged to cause the problem. Note paradoxes related to problem.	Analyze how a problem has changed over time and what it might be like in the future, noting its origin and how factors converged to cause the problem. Adapt solutions from parallel ideas.
Problem Solving (Solutions)	Develop solution ideas with sufficient detail. Develop a model (drawing) to show thinking.	Determine parameters of a problem and at least four solution ideas that fit the parameters.	Determine parameters of a problem and at least four solution ideas with sufficient detail (see Creative Thinking).	Develop solutions from multiple points of view or categories (Who will do what, how will it work) to solve a problem within given parameters.	Develop detailed solutions from multiple points of view or categories (Who will do what, how will it work, addressing assisters and resisters) to solve a problem within given parameters.	Develop multiple, detailed solutions from multiple points of view. Develop sophisticated criteria for determining the best solution from multiple ideas.
Creative Thinking	Develop fluent ideas for a given problem or situation.	Apply fluency and flexibility (e.g., multiple points of view, categories, and application of SCAMPER) to problem solving.	Develop original and elaborate ideas/solutions by adding sufficient detail.	Engage in the creative process (preparation, incubation, illumination, verification) and apply creative processes for the purpose of solving a real-world issue.	Examine how content experts apply the creative process (preparation, incubation, illumination, verification) in various domains.	Fully apply the creative process (preparation, incubation, illumination, verification) to a self-selected study/in-depth investigation.

RESOURCE 4, continued

Grades	K–1	2–3	4–5	6	7	8
Critical Thinking	Identify the strengths and weaknesses of a given idea.	Analyze the strengths and weaknesses of a given idea by explaining long-term consequences.	Use multiple points of view to determine the strengths and weaknesses of a given idea.	Explain how assumptions can lead to erroneous conclusions and note positive and negative implications of an idea.	Evaluate bias in assumptions and evaluate implications using established criteria.	Analyze development of bias within assumptions. Evaluate implications, applying self-generated criteria.
Concept	Relate content to concept generalizations.	Develop concept generalizations from details and categories, and relate content to concept generalizations.	Develop concept generalizations from details and categories, and relate content to concept generalizations, citing evidence to support reasoning.	Articulate how advanced content (including content from other classes) relates to the concept generalizations. Develop questions for research and connect them to macroconcepts or concepts in the discipline.	Connect content-specific principles and theories to concept generalizations. Explore how problems and solutions relate to concept generalizations.	Relate other macro concepts to concept generalizations. Test content-specific principles and theories to concept generalizations (e.g., Do Newton's Laws of Motions support the idea "Structure promotes function"?).

Note. Adapted from *Gifted Education Guide: Sequence of Skills Applied to Advanced Content,* by E. Mofield, 2018, Sumner County Schools. Adapted with permission of the author.

adapted to best use these strategies. In addition, modeling builds capacity in the classroom teacher, developing skills and confidence in applying the strategies to future lessons. For example, during modeling, the gifted education teacher may demonstrate effective follow-up questioning to extend students' critical thinking on the topic to a deeper level, which in turn, builds the skills and competence of the classroom teacher to do the same. Figure 4 shows an example and nonexample of modeling.

Before modeling a strategy, you should engage in the Collaborative Process Model (set a purpose, plan, reflect) as partners; otherwise, modeling is not a true form of collaboration in which both teachers "colabor" in the sharing of ideas. Modeling may be a launching pad of sorts for future collaborative endeavors. Teachers can clarify the shared understanding of each other's role when modeling is used; otherwise, the modeling could be perceived as the gifted education teacher being more powerful than the classroom teacher.

After the modeling, both teachers can reflect on how the students reacted to the lesson, how the strategies impacted student learning, and how students can benefit from similar approaches in future lessons. Both teachers can also discuss how the strategy supported students in learning the content and standards of the lesson. During the postmodeling conversation, the classroom teacher might offer their ideas for next steps in the curriculum sequence and then together, with the gifted education teacher, brainstorm how the modeled strategies might apply.

While the gifted education teacher models a lesson, the classroom teacher could focus on specific ways the gifted education teacher elicits student learning. We have created a guide (Resource 5: Observing Instructional Strategies for Gifted Learners) that can serve to create a focus for the observing teacher. Although not all components of the checklist will be used by the gifted education teacher in one lesson, the components provide a focus for the observing classroom teacher to note that these components are solid instructional practices for teaching gifted students. It can also serve as a guide for reflecting on why these components are beneficial for teaching gifted learners.

We also suggest that before modeling a lesson, the gifted education teacher provides the classroom teacher with the lesson plan to review before the modeling takes place. Then, after the modeling, the two teachers can work together to develop follow-up activities that extend learning over the next few days or weeks.

Modeling a strategy in a classroom can be a good first step before plunging into coteaching with a classroom teacher. Taking these steps in learning from each other can build foundations of trust and develop a balanced perception of power within the partner relationship.

The modeling or demonstration teaching should be used as an opportunity for the classroom teacher to observe student behaviors related to giftedness. By using Resource 5: Observing Instructional Strategies for Gifted Learners, classroom

FIGURE 4

Example and Nonexample of Modeling

Example of Modeling	Nonexample of Modeling
Gifted education teacher models a strategy, such as metaphorical thinking, aligned with the classroom teacher's instructional goals. Classroom teacher observes for specific teaching behaviors and student responses.	Gifted education teacher models a strategy, such as metaphorical thinking, not necessarily aligned with the classroom teacher's instructional goals. Classroom teacher checks email or leaves to make copies.

teachers are invited to observe how students respond to instruction that promotes creative or critical thinking. Again, this continues to build capacity in the classroom teacher by demonstrating and developing contexts that support and challenge gifted learners.

Virtual Collaborative Space

Coplanning lessons in person is not always possible. Further, it is not always possible or necessary to coplan an entire lesson. Sometimes, the gifted education teacher can offer ideas for portions of the lesson, such as developing a tiered assignment or creating in-depth debatable questions for a Socratic seminar. The collaborative process can happen even through email if there is an established shared purpose and input from both parties about the planning process. Through the use of virtual interactive white boards and digital platforms such as Canvas, Google Drive, and Google Classroom, classroom teachers can share prepared lesson plans in advance with the gifted education teacher who can then work to add ABCs (see Chapter 3) to the lesson. This type of coplanning still requires shared decision making, the TEAM frame components, and reflection. In striving for ongoing active professional learning, it is important to create a collaborative space within the digital platform that continues to facilitate "cothinking" throughout the process.

RESOURCE 5
Observing Instructional Strategies for Gifted Learners

Strategies	Evidence in the Lesson
Next-Level Questioning + Would you agree or disagree? Why? + What other information do you need? + How could you represent ____ with a symbol, phrase, body movement, tableau pose, song title, etc.? + What would be another way to ____? + Explain your reasoning. Justify and explain why. + Let's take this a step further . . . what else . . . ? + How would ____ see it differently? + What assumptions are made about ____?	
Engagement Strategies With Advanced Content + Discuss with a partner or small groups using advanced academic vocabulary. + Act out the concept or process. + Debate the controversy (stand on opposite sides of the room) and construct argument with substantial evidence. + Student-student-student talk vs. student-teacher-student.	
Depth, Complexity, Problem Solving + Big ideas (Relate idea to a universal idea, like change, conflict, patterns, systems.) + Paradox (How does this show two contrasting ideas?) + Parallel (How does this relate to ____?) + Multiple perspectives + Abstract thinking (Metaphors, symbolic thinking.) + Connecting ideas (What factors influence ____? What could this lead to?) + Change over time (What do you predict?) + Problem solving around multisided problems; multiple solution ideas	

Strategies	Evidence in the Lesson
Reflective Thinking + Opportunities for students' *aha* celebrations or *uh-oh* clarifications of learning. + Relating content to real-world or self. + Reflecting on applying methods and thinking of the field/discipline (thinking as a historian, mathematician, etc.). + Cementing the concept through application to real-world contexts.	
Teacher Reflection + How did students react to the lesson? + In what ways did the strategies support gifted learners? + What are next steps for instructional planning? + How does this help students make continual progress in their learning?	

Note. Adapted from *Instructional Strategies for Gifted Students Observation Form,* by E. Mofield, 2014, Sumner County Schools. Adapted with permission of the author.

Professional Learning Communities

Beyond coplanning with a specific teacher, professional learning communities offer opportunities to advocate for gifted students. During these collaborative meetings, data are shared among classroom teachers and instructional leaders to make decisions regarding how to help students achieve at high levels. When students are not demonstrating mastery, decisions are made to intervene in order to remediate skill deficits. However, gifted education teachers have an opportunity to shift the collaborative conversation to *extending* the learning for those who have already demonstrated mastery. According the Dufour et al.'s (2010) PLCs framework, helping students achieve at high levels can be accomplished through considering four questions:

1. What do we want students to learn?
2. How will we know if each student has learned it?
3. How will we respond when some students do not learn it?
4. How can we extend and enrich the learning for students who have demonstrated proficiency? (p. 199)

Question 4 is an open door for discussing next steps for the learning of many high-achieving students. These next steps might be to suggest flexible grouping for differentiation, extensions to the curriculum, or tiered assignments with additional depth and complexity. This is an opportunity for data to drive enrichment, not just intervention.

Coplanning Is Cothinking

This chapter highlighted the "how" of coplanning. Coplanning is not a gifted education teacher eagerly saying to a classroom teacher, "I've got a great trick in my bag . . . want to use it?" Although well-intended, this is not reflective of true collaboration in which both teachers shoulder the responsibility in helping students achieve at high levels. Coplanning involves two minds coming together as "thinking partners" for developing engaging instruction for all learners.

Chapter 5

Coteaching Models Adapted for Gifted Education

> If it takes two to tango, why not teach both partners how to dance?
> (Hudson & Glomb, 1997)

Quite simply, coteaching is when two professional educators "co-plan, co-instruct, and co-assess" (Murawski, 2003, p. 10). It is not a one-teacher classroom with an assistant, but a two-teacher classroom, where two teachers are actually teaching and are actively engaged with students. In the context of this book, we emphasize that coteaching is also a way to build capacity in other teachers, especially their capacity to reach and teach gifted learners.

As a part of gifted services, coteaching (through push-in models) might be a provision for gifted programming in addition to other types of services. Coteaching is most manageable if gifted students are in cluster groups so that the gifted education teacher can maximize time and resources by focusing on working with a few teachers. It is also most effective if done consistently with the same coteaching partner over the course of the school year (rather than working sporadically with multiple teachers). The benefits of coteaching for differentiation include the following (Heacox & Cash, 2014; Landrum, 2001; Mofield, 2020a):

+ Differentiation for high-ability learners is more easily managed in the regular classroom (e.g., accelerating and enriching content).

+ Students who need individualized support for acceleration, compacting, or independent study are more likely to receive it.
+ Students who are not necessarily identified as gifted benefit from high-level differentiation strategies.
+ Gifted education is not perceived as an isolated island, but an integrated part of the student's learning experience, even within the regular classroom.
+ Students benefit from the combined expertise of both teachers (expertise in content areas and expertise in designing differentiated learning experiences).
+ The classroom teacher gains an understanding of the needs of gifted students and learns new knowledge for how to address these needs.
+ Students who receive a curriculum matched to their abilities are more likely to make continual progress in their learning.
+ The gifted education teacher can more easily connect academic content into pull-out instruction as a result of coplanning and coteaching with the classroom teacher.

Despite these benefits, unless there is a clear purpose and plan for coteaching, it can easily go awry. Without clear plans, it could look like one teacher leading instruction, while the other teacher is stapling papers or leaning against the back wall. Research on coteaching indicates that the "One Teach, One Assist" model of coteaching is the most often used, but this approach is not necessarily the best way to maximize the use of two professionals in a classroom (e.g., Scruggs et al., 2007). An essential question to consider to determine effectiveness of coteaching is "How is what the two teachers are doing together substantially different and better for students than what one of them would do alone?" (Murawski & Spencer, 2011, p. 96). Coteaching should, indeed, involve both teachers providing substantive instruction together (Murawski & Lochner, 2018).

Preparing for Coteaching

Coteaching has been compared to a marriage of sorts, requiring a balance of trust and openness, even during times of frustration when both individuals don't necessarily see eye to eye. It requires a commitment to shared goals, responsibilities, and decision making. In order for coteaching to really work, it is critical to work through the lens of the TEAM frame (trust, engage, align, maintain) deliberately and intentionally. This is especially important at the beginning of the collaborative relationship. Although the TEAM frame has been explained in previous chapters, here we emphasize specific applications to coteaching.

Trust

Successful coteaching starts with trust. Trust allows for the feeling of struggle without feeling judged, and when embarking on any new endeavor, such as coteaching and differentiation, there can be moments of struggle. If you have a chance to choose a coteaching partner, you might consider choosing a friend or someone you have already developed a positive relationship with. Ideally, choose someone who is eager and willing to take coteaching seriously (even a new teacher). As recommended in the literature, collaboration should be a voluntary process (Landrum, 2002). Even when this is not possible, build trust with your coteacher by sharing a few things about your personal life, how long you have been teaching, and why you are an educator. Follow through with tasks you commit to; do what you say you will do. Building trust requires multiple shared experiences over time. Trust is built during moments of sharing insights about student interests, discussing group dynamics, and retweaking to make last-minute adjustments because of an unannounced schoolwide assembly. Be patient as the foundations for trust are constructed, and acknowledge how credibility is built along the way.

Engage

Engage with each other by tuning in to the strengths, needs, and values of one another through active listening. Deliberately recognize and value each other's strengths and areas of expertise. These strengths should not only be recognized, but also used through the coplanning process for coteaching. Provide praise for the valuable ideas offered, for going the extra mile in preparing materials, for grading papers, or for sharing creative ideas to introduce the lesson. Engage by also asking for help. When you ask for help from each other, you are increasing trust and accountability for the relationship.

Align

Align your beliefs by taking time to reflect on the questions on Resource 6: Developing a Shared Understanding of Beliefs and Values. After each teacher writes out responses, take the time to discuss each question together. Communicating beliefs about teaching philosophies, discipline, grading procedures, and teaching style is foundational to successful coteaching. Time should be allotted to meet and openly discuss each other's opinions on these issues. This is the time to agree, negotiate, or agree to disagree on a number of factors (Heacox & Cash, 2014), coming to a consensus about the best approaches that facilitate student learning.

Developing a Shared Understanding of Beliefs and Values

Personal Reflections on Values, Beliefs, and Practices	
What are your beliefs about gifted learners?	How would you describe your teaching style (traditional to nontraditional)?
How comfortable are you in sharing your classroom space?	How do you handle group work procedures and grading?
How much time do you devote to planning instruction?	What are your expectations of me as your coteaching partner?
How much time are you willing to coplan instruction? When might we coplan instruction?	What are your assumptions about my role in coteaching?
What are your beliefs about grading? What are your grading procedures?	Are there any "nonnegotiables" we must consider?
How do you handle discipline infractions?	How might we promote a sense of "shared" teaching in the classroom? (Use "we/our" language, write both names on the board, avoid talking about "my" students vs. "your" students.)

Maintain

Maintain and sustain successful collaboration by reflecting on the process and outcomes of coteaching. Openly ask for feedback. Provide descriptive feedback to each other in terms of how strategies and ideas affect student learning, rather than in terms of a teacher's style or personality. Additionally, coteaching partners may consider developing a set of norms that spell out the intentions for a successful collaborative relationship (see Figure 5 as an example). It is said that the enemy of accountability is ambiguity (Lencioni, 2003); therefore, there should be clear expectations. Throughout the year, these should be revisited over time. You may ask, "How are we doing in these areas? Is there anything I could be doing to better support you in this coteaching experience?" Teachers may consider using Figure 5 as a guide or developing their own norms to be used throughout the year. These norms should be revisited continuously, allowing you to openly discuss the functionality of the coteaching relationship. It can be a platform for receiving, giving, and using feedback, while keeping each other mutually accountable.

Before embarking on the adventure of coteaching, the gifted education teacher may want to observe the classroom teacher teach and interact with students. This will give the gifted education teacher a sense of the classroom environment and the classroom teacher's instructional style and philosophy in action.

Unraveling Assumptions

Preparing to coteach is an ideal time to uncover and address unspoken or underlying assumptions classroom teachers may have of gifted students. These assumptions might be "gifted students will be fine on their own," "gifted students are well-behaved," and/or "gifted students are high-performing in all content areas." One approach is to talk about your own personal journey into becoming a gifted education teacher. For example, one gifted education teacher shared that she used to think that gifted students did not need any specialized support because there were too many other students who needed help. She spent her entire year teaching fourth grade focusing on remediating skill deficits and "bringing up bubble students," feeling that she completely disregarded the needs of gifted learners. She expressed regret for not addressing the needs of all students in her class, including gifted learners. Other opportunities to address assumptions may come to surface when discussing students' negative behaviors (getting in trouble from being bored in class, underachieving by deliberately refusing to do work). This is an opportunity to address varied beliefs and misconceptions about gifted learners and provide clarity about their unique needs.

FIGURE 5

Coteaching Norms

We will strive to:

+ Contribute a *shared* responsibility in student learning.
+ Work together so that one teacher in not regularly perceived as the "lead" teacher and one teacher as the "assistant."
+ Plan so that both teachers are *teaching* during instruction (not preparing materials, leaning against the wall, or grading papers).
+ Take the time to reflect at the end of lessons to determine next steps.
+ Take turns working with the groups of gifted/high-ability students.
+ Express opinions openly to each other about concerns related to philosophy, teaching style, grading, etc.
+ Not blame one another for problems; rather, we will work collaboratively to solve problems.
+ Use "we/our" language when interacting with students to promote "shared teaching" (e.g., "We want you to think about . . .").
+ Guard against one person doing "all of the work." Both will contribute to shared planning, instruction, and assessment.
+ Other considerations:

_____   _____

Classroom Teacher   Gifted Education Teacher

Models of Coteaching

Friend and Cook (2017) described six classic models for coteaching. These models are typically used to teach in the contexts of meeting the needs of students with disabilities or English language learners (ELLs). These models have also been adapted and applied in gifted education contexts (Fogarty & Tschida, 2018; Hughes & Murawski, 2001). Here we provide examples and adaptations of their uses for supporting and extending academic challenge for gifted learners.

Tango Teaching (Team Teaching)

Traditionally, Team Teaching (Friend & Cook, 2017) is when two teachers are teaching side by side. We like to think of it as Tango Teaching, where two teachers are directly in step with each other, one ready with a step or strategy for adding challenge to instruction. The classroom teacher might introduce the lesson, while the gifted education teacher adds a debatable issue or high-level thinking questions.

Example. Both teachers stand in front of the class to introduce a unit on the American Revolutionary War. The classroom teacher asks the essential question: "Is revolution rebellion?" Students may respond from Loyalist and Patriot perspectives. Each teacher takes turns eliciting responses from all students, writing responses on the board. The teachers may provide a humorous competition between themselves, one representing a Loyalist and eliciting responses, while the other represents a Patriot. To challenge students' thinking, students can be asked to state underlying assumptions, provide evidence for their points of view, and explain the long-term implications for their points of view (see Chapter 6 for further explanation).

Tier Teaching (Parallel Teaching)

In the classic coteaching model of Parallel Teaching, each teacher teaches the same content to different groups of students. This way, there are more opportunities for students to respond in smaller groups, compared to participating in whole-group instruction. This variation for gifted coteaching has been described as Tier Teaching (Hughes & Murawski, 2001). Each teacher teaches the same content, but one teacher delivers instruction with an additional tier or layer of challenge.

Example. Each teacher may conduct a Socratic seminar with students. One teacher works with students who need a more challenging text, while the other teacher works with students on a grade-level text. Both groups have opportunities for critical thinking because both teachers provide high-level questions during the Socratic seminar, but the grade-level group may require more scaffolding for high-level thinking.

Carousel Teaching (Station Teaching)

Station Teaching traditionally involves students rotating through different stations to learn and apply content. Both teachers teach at a station, and other stations are set up for group or individual work. We have named Station Teaching, Carousel Teaching in contexts of teaching gifted students. Stations can be differentiated for interest and readiness levels (stations provide movement up toward more challenge or movement down, like on a carousel). For gifted learners (or those who need additional challenge), the stations can be vertically differentiated to address readiness, so both the gifted education teacher and classroom teacher can provide differentiation at their stations.

Example. A middle school English language arts class is studying poetry by Edgar Allan Poe. At one station, students examine primary source letters from Poe to various individuals in his life. After reading these documents, students make conclusions about who the person "Annabel Lee" was in Poe's life. The teacher at this station facilitates critical thinking through a primary source analysis to guide students to develop conclusions. To differentiate for the high-readiness group, students look at the primary source through elements of reasoning (see Chapter 6). In another station, facilitated by a teacher, students engage in a literary analysis about "The Raven." To add complexity, the teacher guides students in comparing its theme to another poem. At another station, students examine illustrative pieces of art developed for "The Raven." Students study the text and determine which pictures relate to specific stanzas, justifying their thinking with evidence from the text. In another station, students listen to a brief podcast about Poe's life and reflect on how his life experiences impacted his writing.

Scout Teaching (One Teach, One Observe)

The traditional One Teach, One Observe is adapted here as Scout Teaching. This involves one teacher presenting a lesson while the other teacher observes student learning and behavior. Specifically, the "Scout" (the observing teacher) focuses on identifying evidence of high potential: strong problem-solving skills, creativity, and abstract thinking. The "Scout" teacher may also track student progress and the development of specific strengths. As a result, students may be referred for formal gifted identification.

Stretch Teaching (One Teach, One Support)

In Friend and Cook's (2017) One Teach, One Assist coteaching model, one teacher teaches while the other teacher assists students who may need additional support to access the content of the lesson. In the context of gifted education, Stretch Teaching is used to enrich the content. While one teacher teaches, the other teacher may extend student thinking by asking more challenging questions, such as divergent questions, eliciting more flexible and elaborate responses that "stretch" their thinking. We see Scout and Stretch Teaching working well together; as one teacher provides a "stretch" in instruction, the other teacher can "scout."

Example. This example is a combination of Scout Teaching and Stretch Teaching. A classroom teacher may be leading a lesson about the engineering design process. Students are asked to apply the engineering process to design better athletic equipment (e.g., making a football helmet safer). During the lesson, as one teacher continues to teach the lesson, one teacher looks for evidence of students' critical thinking, problem solving, creativity, etc., through Scout Teaching. The teacher may also ask follow-up questions in small groups that continue to extend thinking as Stretch Teaching (e.g., What else could you do? What might you minimize or maximize? How would this work?). See Chapter 6 for using "Stretch Prompts" for specific questions that extend students' thinking.

Safari Teaching (Alternative Teaching)

According to Friend and Cook's (2017) model, alternative teaching occurs when one teacher teaches regular curricular content while the coteacher teaches something different (to reteach, review, or reinforce skills). In the context of coteaching for gifted learners, we refer to this as Safari Teaching. For students who have already demonstrated mastery of content, the gifted education teacher may work on different accelerated content altogether or on an enrichment activity that extends the regular curriculum. This "safari" is a short trip away from the regular path, providing opportunities for student exploration through extensions.

Example. The classroom teacher may provide direct instruction on ratio and proportions. Most students need support and practice with making conversions and cross multiplying, but some students have already demonstrated mastery of these skills on a preassessment. These students may then work with the gifted education teacher on learning about the golden ratio and its relationship to the Fibonacci sequence. Students may be asked to find examples of the Fibonacci sequence and golden ratio in nature through a photo scavenger hunt. We caution that all students should have opportunities to explore their interests as they relate to the curriculum, and all students should have exposure to curricular extensions. Safari Teaching should not just be perceived by students as being in the "fun group." This approach facilitates compacting for groups of students who have already demonstrated proficiency in learning. It also works well for accelerating content and working on a separate curriculum.

Table 13 provides nonexamples and points of clarity for each coteaching model.

Other Considerations

During one class session, it is likely that a number of coteaching methods are suitable. Certainly, more than one method can be used during a lesson. For example, the lesson may start out with Tango Teaching, where teachers introduce the topic or issue together, and then lead into Tiered Teaching. In Carousel Teaching, the gifted teacher might implement Safari Teaching at the station because students already know the content. Flexibility is a key to coteaching. Changing routines is important so that you and your students are not stuck in a rut and that the gifted education

TABLE 13
Clarifying Models of Coteaching

Model	Nonexample	Clarifying Point
Tango Teaching	One teacher leads discussion while the other teacher only writes responses on the board.	Both teachers should be teaching the content together so that there is no clear "lead" teacher.
Tier Teaching	The classroom teacher only asks low-level questions to their group while the gifted education teacher asks high-level questions.	Both teachers should be providing high-level questions; the gifted education teacher may provide even more depth and complexity within the questions and include higher level texts. The gifted education teacher may also work with the grade-level group.
Carousel Teaching	Students work on worksheets at each station. Teachers do not level up or down in response to student readiness at the stations.	Stations are more than opportunities for group work on a worksheet. At teacher stations, teachers add vertical differentiation (more rigor for those who need it) while working directly with students.
Scout and Stretch Teaching	One teacher teaches while the other teacher assists in taking attendance.	Although there are times when the coteacher may take attendance to facilitate efficiency in classroom routines, this is not a coteaching method. Scout and Stretch Teaching involve discovering student strengths and developing them.
Safari Teaching	The "high" group of students works with the gifted education teacher all semester on preparing for a competition (e.g., History Day, Invention Convention, etc.).	Safari teaching should relate directly to curricular content, taking it a step further. Flexible grouping decisions should be made on an ongoing basis through the use of formative assessments.

teacher and classroom teacher work with various groups of students (the gifted teacher does not always need to work with gifted students). We emphasize, too, that grouping decisions for tiered instruction are made based on continuous assessment data. This means that groups will likely change over time. Gifted students are not gifted in all content areas and will have varied skill levels in different domains. Just because a student may be labeled as gifted does not necessarily mean they need the differentiation applied in coteaching in every situation in every lesson.

Shared Instructional Decision Making

Coteaching requires coplanning, a process involving shared decisions about instruction. "Winging it" by asking "what are we doing today?" will not lead to successful outcomes. Table 14 is a model that can be used to discuss how each teacher contributes to the planning process and how coteaching models might be implemented within the lesson. Note that it is not necessary for each teacher to have a role for every planning question, but the overall plan creates a path that allows for shared responsibility in teaching all students in the classroom. Resource 7: Planning for Coteaching is a template that includes these questions and roles.

Reflection After Coteaching

After coteaching, genuinely reflect and touch base about the cotaught lesson. This reflection allows for the "M" part of TEAM—maintenance of the collaborative relationship to be strengthened—and can provide a context for disagreements or conflicts to be addressed in a nonthreatening way. Some questions to guide reflective discussion include:

+ How do we know students were engaged?
+ What students need continued support?
+ Did this go as we expected? Why, or why not?
+ If we were to conduct this lesson again, what might we do differently?
+ How did we apply each other's expertise?
+ What did you observe that I may have missed?
+ What concerns do you have?
+ What did we do better, together?
+ What can we do better, together, next time?
+ To what extent did we truly coteach, both fulfilling the role of the teacher in the classroom?

As partners grow in their coteaching relationship, they can develop specific goals for improving the power of collaborative teaching. Together, you might consider the use of microteaching, which is "the opportunity to work on one or a few identified isolated skills, which allows for reflection" (Murawski & Lochner, 2018, p. 137). For example, as a team, you can videotape a microlesson and reflect on whether together you demonstrated the targeted skill. This would be followed by developing steps for further refinement. Dialogues around the coteachers' strengths and limitations can also take place within learning communities with other coteach-

TABLE 14
Planning for Coteaching: Shared Decision-Making Example

Planning Questions	Gifted Teacher's Role	Regular Education Teacher's Role
How will we preassess?	+ Score the pretest.	+ Develop pretest to measure what students should know, do, and understand.
How will we group students?	+ Work with students who made a 90% or more, who will be grouped together during Tiered Teaching.	+ Work with students who have not met 90% mastery.
What coteaching approaches will we use throughout the lesson? + Tango Teaching + Tiered Teaching + Scout/Stretch Teaching + Carousel Teaching + Safari Teaching	+ Scout Teach while the classroom teacher presents initial material. + Stretch Teaching: Add in questions about change over time and ethics during debate. + Tiered Teaching: Use a more advanced resource with the advanced group.	+ Lead a quick debate on an issue for the whole group. + Tiered Teaching: Use a standards-based lesson and resources.
What differentiation strategies will we use to advance the content, build the buy-in, and create a challenge?	+ Gather advanced resources to use for the lesson. + Add elements of Kaplan's depth and complexity in tiered instruction and assignment (see Chapter 6).	+ Add reflection questions to relate content to students' lives. Gather a variety of multimedia resources to relate to students' experiences and interests.
How will we assess student learning?	+ Collect data (work samples) from high-tiered group (formative). + Create differentiated rubrics for the product (summative).	+ Collect data (work samples) from grade-level group (formative). + Develop initial ideas for product choices (summative).
After the lesson: What are our next steps?	+ Continue to make observations regarding Student C, who has shown evidence of gifted behaviors. Note that this may lead to a gifted referral.	+ Plan for remediation for those who have not demonstrated sufficient progress. + Reflect on group dynamics and make necessary adjustments.

Planning for Coteaching: Shared Decision Making

Planning Questions	Gifted Teacher's Role	Regular Education Teacher's Role
How will we preassess?		
How will we group students?		
What coteaching approaches will we use throughout the lesson? + Tango Teaching + Tiered Teaching + Scout/Stretch Teaching + Carousel Teaching + Safari Teaching		
What differentiation strategies will we use to advance the content, build the buy-in, and create a challenge?		
How will we assess student learning?		
After the lesson: What are our next steps?		

ing partners. Such learning communities can offer collegial support for improving the craft of coteaching.

Diving In

Are you ready to get your feet wet? Where do you start? Coteaching involves consistent planning for layers of differentiation, but we want to emphasize that this does not have to be complicated. Start small. First steps might include coteaching a lesson with familiar content and strategies you are both comfortable using. Give each other permission for the process to feel awkward at first, but persevere through the discomfort and make adjustments along the way.

Acknowledge and expect that there will be conflict through this process, but know that the conflict may provide context for your coteaching relationship to grow and thrive. Teams that avoid conflict avoid the opportunity to debate and disagree on important ideas (Lencioni, 2003) that may lead to important decisions about what's best for students. If you can apply the TEAM frame, then it can be safe and even beneficial to experience and work through conflict, strengthening the power of your collaborative relationship.

Whether you're ready to dive in or just dip your toe into the water, remember that successful coteaching necessitates at least one teacher to be wholly committed and devoted to continuing the process, even through frustration and difficulty. Coteaching can feel awkward at first, and like any new skill, it takes considerable commitment and practice. Over time, as the coteaching relationship develops, you will become more comfortable taking risks in developing flexible approaches to instruction. As emphasized previously, coteaching is also a vehicle for both partners to engage in sustained professional learning together, as both teachers learn from each other's expertise and arrive at new possibilities through shared decision making. Coteaching can also involve peer coaching (see Chapter 8), where teachers can openly dialogue and reflect on fine-tuning practices related to self-selected goals. Finally, don't forget the reason behind this endeavor—with the development of trust over time, the coteaching team can create invaluable opportunities that develop students' gifts and talents.

Chapter 6

Strategies for Vertical Differentiation

This chapter provides strategies to further enhance classroom instruction through vertical differentiation (see Chapter 3). These include the use of critical thinking process models that are easily integrated across multiple grade levels and content areas to tier existing lessons and further differentiate learning. Beyond sharing these strategies with classroom teachers and other various collaborative partners, we emphasize the value of "colaboring" to make decisions together on how they might be used and applied to advanced content.

Elevating Classroom Practice

As you begin to meet with your colleagues, remember to take time to celebrate the strengths and contributions that classroom teachers bring to the table. As a gifted education teacher, it is extremely difficult to be an expert in every content area across every grade level. Recognize the specialties that classroom teachers contribute to the collaborative process, and acknowledge the successful strategies already being implemented within their classrooms. From here, continue to build upon the TEAM frame (especially with "engage"), and also integrate additional layers of challenge into what the classroom teacher has planned. For example, the classroom teacher might already be using lessons that incorporate engaging strategies, such as Socratic seminars, gallery walks, debates, simulations, or jigsaws, to name a few. Work to increase the level of challenge for such activities through strategies discussed later in this chapter or through additional flexible methods of differentiation, such as the following:

+ Have students take on different perspectives while providing insights, arguments, and/or feedback throughout the lesson.
+ Provide opportunities for students to identify assumptions that were made or could be made throughout the content focus.
+ Differentiate reading levels of text utilized as part of each strategy.

Ready, Set, Now What?

Before delving into the various strategies, the collaborative team should identify the instructional goal for the lesson and seek to challenge all learners. Consider the following when exploring which strategy to implement:

+ **What are the needs of the students?** This includes both their academic and affective needs. Choose a strategy that addresses what you know about students' academic levels of readiness through pre- and formative assessments and provide an opportunity for students to work through their areas of strength. For instance, certain students respond to strategies that are more creative and open-ended, whereas others thrive on more structured and linear strategies that provide a distinct progression of thought.
+ **What are the measurable outcomes?** While choosing a strategy, identify how students will demonstrate their understanding of the content. Whether this is through completing components of the learning activity itself or other ways such as written reflections, active participation in discussions, or authentic products, the chosen strategies and learning activities can serve as the conduit to measure the desired learning targets.
+ **How will the environment impact the desired outcome(s)?** Some strategies require ample room for students to spread out and work in groups; others might require open wall space. If coteaching is a consideration, successful strategy selection should consider which option is best for the desired coteaching model (e.g., Tango, Tier, Carousel, Scout and Stretch, or Safari Teaching; see Chapter 5), each requiring varying levels of flexibility.
+ **What resources are easily accessible?** Ask yourself: Do your students have access to technology? Are needed resources available from the library? Are there dry erase boards for your students to use? Although there are always ways to problem solve through these access issues, take the time to think

through what types of resources are needed to successfully implement the chosen strategy.

+ **How will the standards be addressed?** Regardless of the chosen strategy, teaching the standards remains a priority. While collaborating on which strategy will work best to differentiate for gifted learners in the regular classroom, take time to address which strategy aligns optimally with integrating the desired standards. This will not only make the differentiation process more seamless, but also streamline the focus of the lesson itself.

Now, it's time to strategize! Many of the instructional strategies in this chapter are based on creative or critical thinking models and should be applied with the presentation of advanced content in order to most appropriately challenge gifted learners.

Elements of Reasoning

Paul and Elder's (2019) elements of reasoning is a model used to develop critical thinking skills, specifically applied to analyze, evaluate, and improve one's thinking. This model can be used to teach students how to reason with "parts of thinking" or "elements." These elements include questions, purpose, points of view, assumptions, concepts, information, inferences, and implications. By incorporating this model in questioning, reflection, debates, and other class activities, students learn to develop reasoned judgments, evaluate points of view and biases, make valid inferences, and construct logical arguments. Questions related to the elements of reasoning include the following:

+ **Question:** What is the problem, issue, or key question I want to answer?
+ **Purpose:** What is the ultimate goal or reason to examine the issue?
+ **Point of view:** What is my point of view on the issue? What is another stakeholder's point of view on the issue?
+ **Assumptions:** What do we believe, value, or take for granted about the issue being explored? What are others' assumptions about the same issue?
+ **Concepts/ideas:** What are the terms, principles, theories, or definitions being used?
+ **Information/evidence:** What data or evidence is there to support my reasoning?
+ **Inferences/interpretations:** What conclusions can be drawn based on the data?
+ **Implications/consequences:** What might happen as a result?

Depending on the purpose of the lesson and student readiness levels, all or just a few of the elements of reasoning can be integrated into a lesson to develop students' critical thinking. This model is far more than just a graphic organizer to categorize one's thinking, it is a mental model to develop reasoning skills around a topic of study.

Examples of Practice

Exploring Ethical Dilemmas. While developing a lesson focused on the novel *The House of the Scorpion* by Nancy Farmer, a classroom teacher and gifted education teacher collaborate on how Paul and Elder's (2019) elements of reasoning can be used to help students examine the ethical considerations of human cloning in relation to the novel. In doing so, greater connections are made for understanding the theme. For the objectives of this lesson, the teachers elect to focus on the purpose, point of view, evidence, and implications of this topic.

After coplanning the lesson and finding multiple articles regarding the advancement of somatic cell cloning, the classroom teacher uses the jigsaw strategy to have students process and share the information found within each article. The classroom teacher then asks the class a question related to the issue: "Should somatic cell cloning research be allowed to continue?" To answer the question, students critically think about the information through some of the elements of reasoning in the following manner:

+ **Purpose:** Students begin by identifying the purpose behind this research. Responses might include: Alzheimer's patients desperately need a cure, scientists want notoriety and wealth, and people want to live longer.

+ **Point of view:** Students explore the different points of view involved with the issue. These could include Alzheimer's patients, scientists, or animal rights activists.

+ **Information/evidence:** Students gather evidence from the articles to answer the issue question, citing specific reasons why or why not somatic cell cloning research should continue.

+ **Implications/consequences:** Students examine the positive and negative implications of allowing somatic stem cell research. A positive implication is that the research could lead to a potential cure for Alzheimer's patients, while a negative implication is that animals would be used for testing and could die.

+ **Concepts/ideas:** Students identify the major abstract ideas used to understand this issue—such as bioethics, regenerative medicine, human rights, and what it means to be "human"—and consider assumptions made about these concepts from various perspectives.

Helpful Hints

+ Create a "Paul's Wall" by using duct tape to create a web showing the elements of reasoning on a classroom wall or bulletin board. As a formative assessment measure, students can write their thoughts on sticky notes and place them in the appropriate sections to demonstrate levels of understanding.
+ Synthesize multiple sources of information through the elements of reasoning. For example, students could use the elements of reasoning to prepare for a debate.
+ Use the elements of reasoning to coplan Socratic seminars. In doing so, combine the elements into questions. For example: How do the details (evidence) support the author's point of view? What assumptions do we make about this concept/idea (e.g., When we think about the word *freedom,* what do we assume? What beliefs do we take for granted?)?
+ Use the elements of reasoning as a model for teaching students how to construct valid arguments in writing or debate. Beyond supporting a claim through a point of view with evidence, students can learn to build logical arguments using all parts of thinking (e.g., addressing assumptions, closely examining the meaning of concepts, noting other points of view, discussing positive and negative implications, evaluating interpretations of data, etc.).

Depth and Complexity Thinking Tools

Based on how disciplinarians think about content, these tools help students examine data and make connections within and across disciplines (Kaplan, 2009). The icons associated with the thinking tools are widely accessible online.

+ Depth thinking prompts include language of the discipline, details, patterns, rules, trends, unanswered questions, ethics, and big ideas that form the content of the topic.
+ Complexity thinking prompts include change over time, connection with other disciplines, and multiple points of view.
+ Content imperatives prompts can be used with depth and complexity to add additional layers of complexity. These include parallels, origins, contributions, paradoxes, and convergence.

Although all students benefit from analyzing academic concepts through the depth and complexity thinking tools, combining multiple tools and incorporating higher order thinking (e.g., analysis, evaluation, and synthesis) increase the level of challenge for gifted learners.

Examples of Practice

Questioning Across Content Disciplines. When coplanning for instruction, Table 15 provides examples to share with the classroom teacher on how the thinking tools might be used to add layers of depth and complexity to questioning. After introducing the tools with the following examples, continue to brainstorm other ways they might apply to a classroom teacher's specific grade level and content area.

"Iconic" Renaissance. After learning more about Kaplan's (2009) thinking tools, collaboration with a classroom teacher might focus on developing a lesson that incorporates greater depth and complexity. The gifted education teacher and classroom teacher might begin collaboration by looking at the current summative assessment tasks. These might include:

+ Write a newspaper article about the importance of the Renaissance.
+ Develop a podcast that explains how the Crusades led to the Renaissance.
+ Create a museum exhibit that depicts the differences in Renaissance art.

After reading through the various tasks, the gifted education teacher and classroom teacher discuss how Kaplan's (2009) tools can be used to add layers of depth and complexity to these same tasks. Collaboratively, the two teachers create the more rigorous options:

+ Write a newspaper article about the importance of the Renaissance. Include *perspectives* from Leonardo da Vinci, Queen Elizabeth I, Michelangelo, Andreas Vesalius, and William Shakespeare. Explain the different *contributions* that they made, how they affected multiple *disciplines*, and ultimately, how they *changed the course* of history.
+ Create a podcast highlighting how the Crusades led to the Renaissance, and explain how this *parallels* a similar *pattern* with the dawning of the Age of Exploration, as well as other major eras in Western civilization. Identify and explain the significance of a common factor found across each of these historic periods.
+ Create a museum exhibit that depicts the differences in Renaissance art from Italy, France, and Germany. Include how the *big ideas* of each region led to varied artistic *trends* showing different *details* within the artwork.

Helpful Hints

+ Create "thinking tool" rolling cubes or laminated cards to challenge students to articulate and explain their thinking throughout any lesson.
+ Challenge students to respond to questions by referencing the various thinking tools. For example, when asked what new scientific insights were

TABLE 15
Adding Depth and Complexity Tools to Questions

Content Area	Basic Question	Added Combination of Depth, Complexity, and Content Imperatives *With* Higher Order Thinking
English Language Arts	How is the theme (*big idea*) in *The Giver* like other stories we have read?	(Analysis) What factors *converged* for Jonas in *The Giver* to *change over time*? How is the *big idea* in *The Giver* a *parallel* to current issues?
Math	How would you explain the *pattern* shown on the graph?	(Evaluation) Do the *trends* in the data create potential *ethical issues*? How do these issues relate to the *big idea* being communicated?
Science	What has led to gorillas becoming an endangered species (*origin*)?	(Synthesis) What *patterns converged* to change the *trend* in the population, and what might reverse the trend?
Social Studies	Explain the significance of Homer's *Odyssey* with supporting *details*.	(Analysis) Explain how the epic of Homer's *Odyssey* shows a *pattern* that *parallels* with India's ancient epics.

learned, a student could respond with, "By analyzing the *details* of our evidence, we discovered *patterns* that helped us uncover scientific principles."

+ Use the thinking tools in long-term assignments or independent investigations to help students transfer concepts within a discipline. For example, ask students how historical perspectives of the Earth's placement in the universe are enhanced by explaining how *multiple perspectives* of the Earth's placement in the solar system have *changed over time*. Then, continue to have students explore what other *controversies* in science have *changed over time* and how they might continue to change in the future.

Double Fishbone

Although the double fishbone might look like just another graphic organizer (see Figure 6), this strategy is successful in helping gifted students delve deeper into their analytical thinking. Through this strategy (from Juntune, 2013), students write the issue, problem, or situation in the center square and complete the "fishbones" to the left with direct and indirect influences of the problem and the "fishbones" to the right with the multiple effects of the problem, including short-term, long-term, pos-

FIGURE 6
Double Fishbone

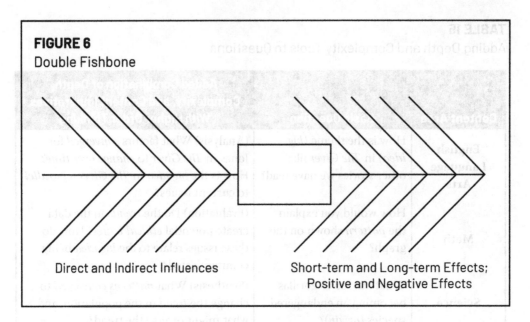

Direct and Indirect Influences

Short-term and Long-term Effects;
Positive and Negative Effects

itive, and negative effects. In addition, the double fishbone offers the opportunity for gifted learners to explore how the cause-effect relationship is impacted through different perspectives and categories. For example, students reading a nonfiction text about business and commerce might explore how the closing of large, indoor shopping malls affects other local businesses, social relationships, and technology, with each category creating new "effects" or implications.

This strategy is particularly useful when collaborating with teachers on problem-based learning tasks, debates, or reflection on simulations. The creative problem-solving process (Treffinger & Isaksen, 2005) is often used to guide students through analyzing and solving a problem. Through this process, students learn to define the problem by identifying the underlying root cause of an issue. Through the deep analysis of multiple causes and effects of the problem, students can better understand a problem or issue before developing creative solutions. In some situations, students can use multiple sources to research the problem or issue more in depth and continue to add to their fishbone.

Examples of Practice

Safari Teaching and Carousel Teaching. The double fishbone can work well while coteaching using Safari Teaching. For example, the classroom teacher and the gifted education teacher both explore the same guiding question ("How are plastics in the ocean harming marine life?"), but each teacher uses a different instructional approach. Based on student readiness, the classroom teacher shares a short informational video with students who are working at grade level, and then the students begin researching answers to the guiding question from preselected websites. Concurrently, the gifted education teacher uses the double fishbone to create a more complex task with the same guiding question. In this case, the learners needing additional challenge research multiple reasons why plastics harm ocean life (on the left) and then write out all of the effects on the right. Their writing might include effects to the food chain, which in turn might affect the health of humans. Additionally, it might include economic effects for local fishermen, effects on biodiversity, and possible extinction of various marine life.

This strategy also works well in other contexts, such as Carousel Teaching. For example, at one station the gifted education teacher might work with advanced learners to understand the characterization methods used to develop the main character, specifically how plot events impact the character. Using the double fishbone, students write out all of the causes (direct and indirect) for an incident in the story and all of the effects and implications (on the right). Through this discussion, students can determine how the incident affects the character's thoughts, emotions, realizations, and interactions with others. The gifted education teacher may then use these insights to guide students to understand how the interaction of the character and the incident contributes to understanding the theme in the story. At another station, students might work independently on a Venn diagram, comparing and contrasting characters within the story (e.g., actions, motives, beliefs). At a third station, the classroom teacher might work with students who need additional support with identifying the theme of the story through a teacher-led activity.

Helpful Hints

+ Have several double fishbone templates laminated or in plastic sheet protectors for students to write on with dry erase markers at any time. The more students are exposed to this strategy, the more they gravitate toward it when analyzing, exploring, or problem solving different situations.

+ Raise the level of challenge by having students create more "fishbones" stemming from their identified causes and effects. For example, if students are thinking about the multiple effects of a required minimum wage, one effect might be that businesses may rely more on self-service computers in order to save money in hiring individuals. The effect of this might be that fewer social interactions might take place in fast food restaurants or stores. These "effects of effects" would be written in as extra fishbones, stemming from the original effect.

+ Provide students with various categories to think through multiple causes and effects. These might include health, economics, culture, geography, emotions, communication, etc. Additionally, students may consider various perspectives of the problem, which may elicit ideas for additional causes and effects.

+ Use the double fishbone to help students analyze document-based questions (DBQs) often used in Pre-AP or AP classes by signifying the causes and implications of historical change. For example, after examining primary and secondary sources related to the Russian Revolution, students indicate multiple causes: the lack of leadership from Tsar Nicholas II, public strikes, and lack of preparedness for World War I as contributing factors for the Russian Revolution. Multiple implications include: Russian society's mistrust and lack of respect for the tsar, a growing movement prepared to struggle and triumph over oppression, and the psychological effects of Russian soldiers being inadequately prepared for war. Such analysis would prepare students to answer a guiding question within a DBQ: What were the significant political, economic, and ideological principles that contributed to the Russian Revolution?

Six Thinking Hats

The Six Thinking Hats strategy (de Bono, 1985/2016) allows students to apply critical thinking by examining information from different perspectives by figuratively "wearing" different colored hats. Students focus these different perspectives on the same common problem or area of focus, and in doing so, develop a deeper level of conceptual understanding. These "hats" include the following perspectives:

+ **White hat (facts):** figures, objectives, data, statistics
+ **Red hat (feelings):** intuition, hunches, emotions, impulses
+ **Black hat (cautions):** judgments, criticisms, negative views
+ **Yellow hat (benefits):** positives, values, benefits, optimism
+ **Blue hat (process):** organizer, control, conductor, implementer
+ **Green hat (creativity):** new ideas, alternatives, modifications, variations

Whether students are annotating an article, examining scientific data, or delving into a historical simulation, de Bono's Six Thinking Hats expand students' critical thinking through multiple perspectives and increase the complexity of a lesson. This strategy is built upon the concept of parallel thinking, meaning all perspectives focus on the same problem or content area.

Examples of Practice

Differentiated Debate. De Bono's (1985/2016) Six Thinking Hats are easily integrated into already established instructional strategies. For example, a gifted education teacher might collaborate with middle school science teachers on coplanning a differentiated debate on colonizing Mars as a solution to the overpopulation of Earth. After already successfully differentiating texts based on student readiness levels, the science teachers collaborate with the gifted education teacher to further differentiate an upcoming debate. The gifted education teacher helps them integrate multiple perspectives through the Six Thinking Hats. In knowing that this strategy incorporates parallel thinking, each debate group utilizes de Bono's six perspectives to develop the most viable arguments for their side. One possible approach might include:

1. Divide students into debate groups.
2. Provide students with the debate proposition: Colonizing Mars is a solution to the overpopulation of Earth.
3. Provide differentiated texts to students based on readiness levels. In addition to classroom texts, other sources can be used, such as Newsela and CommonLit.
4. Have each group highlight and annotate their reading selections based on one of the hats in de Bono's multiple perspectives.
5. Use the insights gained through the different perspectives to develop stronger arguments for debate.

Persuasion Through Perspectives. After learning about the Six Thinking Hats at a recent faculty meeting, a second-grade teacher meets with the gifted education teacher to coplan a persuasive writing unit for her gifted cluster class. Collaboratively, the two teachers develop a lesson using the mentor text *I Wanna Iguana* by Karen Kaufman Orloff. As the lesson begins, the classroom teacher involves the class in analysis by asking, "How did Alex use multiple perspectives to persuade his mom that he should have an iguana?" Table 16 includes potential questions and possible responses for this teaching scenario. Although this is just one example, similar questions can easily be applied to any text.

Once the class examines how the different perspectives are represented in the mentor text, the classroom teacher guides the class in a discussion about how examining different perspectives is an important aspect in persuasive writing. The teacher might ask:

+ Why is it important to think through multiple perspectives in persuasive writing?
+ Which hat is the most important when trying to persuade someone? Why?

TABLE 16
De Bono's Six Thinking Hats Teaching Example

How did Alex use multiple perspectives to persuade his mom that he should have an iguana?	
Potential Questions	Possible Responses
White Hat (facts, figures, data, etc.) + Alex tried to provide his mom with facts about why an iguana could be a good pet; what did he include? + The white hat would also have us think through the cost of something. Did Alex ever mention anything about money?	+ Iguanas are quiet. + It takes 15 years before iguanas become large. + Alex would pay for the iguana's lettuce with his allowance.
Red Hat (feelings, emotions, etc.) + What did Alex say to his mom that would make her feel how important it was for him to have an iguana? + How did Alex make his mom feel guilty if he didn't get the iguana?	+ Alex said he needed a friend *now*. + Alex said the iguana could be the brother he always wanted . . . one that did more than burp and poop. + Alex said that Stinky's dog, Lurch, would eat the iguana if he didn't get it, and he asked his mom, "You don't want that to happen, do you?"
Black Hat (cautions, negative views, etc.) + In *I Wanna Iguana*, who made the most statements from the black hat perspective? Why do you think it was like this? + Was there ever a time when Alex responded with the black hat perspective?	+ The mom's responses were mostly from the black hat perspective because she was arguing *against* Alex's persuasive arguments. + When Alex responded to already having a brother, he negatively stated that his brother just burps and poops.
Yellow Hat (positives, benefits, etc.) + How would Alex benefit from an iguana? + What is positive about having an iguana as a pet?	+ Alex would have a friend. + Iguanas are quiet. + The iguana is so small, the mom wouldn't even know he was there.
Blue Hat (organizer, implementer, etc.) + We know that the blue hat helps us manage the process of our thinking, so when we think of Alex, how did he let his mom know that he was ready to manage having an iguana as a pet?	+ Alex let his mom know that he had already planned that the iguana's cage would fit on the top of his dresser. + Alex stated he would give his iguana food and water and clean his cage. + Alex said he would pay for the lettuce.
Green Hat (creativity, alternatives, etc.) + How did Alex let his mom know that an iguana is a better alternative than his brother?	+ Alex let his mom know that he could teach an iguana tricks and things, unlike he could with his brother.

+ How does the audience you are trying to persuade impact which perspectives are most important?
+ How does the topic impact which perspectives are most important?
+ How do the different perspectives help to identify important stakeholders in the persuasive argument?
+ Why is it important to think through the perspective of the black hat if you are not planning to use that in your writing?

Through these culminating, reflective discussions, students gain a stronger conceptual understanding of how to construct strong persuasive arguments.

Helpful Hints

+ Integrate the Six Thinking Hats with the jigsaw strategy by having student groups "jigsaw" a text, statistical representation, piece of art, or other academic selection based on each of the different perspectives. Students then regroup with students from different thinking hats to participate in discussions where each member only responds or shares insights from their assigned perspective.
+ Have colored laminated hats with short question stems ready to distribute to students during any type of discussion or examination of new material. Each student would respond to the learning activity through the perspective of their assigned hat.
+ Create a "Six Hats" rolling cube that can be used to encourage flexibility of thinking in classroom discussions through any content area.
+ Provide additional challenge by providing students with multiple hats to process information simultaneously.

Dimensions of Creative Thinking

Dimensions of creative thinking is a model useful for developing divergent thinking skills. In contrast to convergent thinking in which students arrive at one answer, divergent thinking involves thinking of as many ideas as possible in an open-ended format. Divergent thinking is developed through the four dimensions of creativity: fluency, flexibility, originality, and elaboration (Guilford, 1986):
+ Fluency refers to the number of ideas, concepts, solutions, possibilities, etc., that a student is able to express.

+ Flexibility examines the connections and categories that stem from ideas: The more diverse and varied the ideas, the more flexible the thinking.
+ Originality includes uncommon and out-of-the-ordinary ideas. Generated ideas that are more unique represent greater originality.
+ Elaboration is the process of adding details, explanations, and clarifications to the generated ideas.

Depending on the focus of the lesson, all four components do not have to be implemented together. For example, collaborative partners might focus solely on increasing student fluency through a brainstorming activity or improving elaboration during writer's workshop. As with any instructional strategy, it should be used purposefully and directly apply to content.

Examples of Practice

Dimensions of Creativity Through Concept Mapping. Concept mapping is a valuable instructional tool across multiple contexts, including pre- and postassessments and prewriting. It can be easily integrated as part of Scout Teaching (observing students who demonstrate exceptional skills in a particular area), when teachers use concept mapping through the four dimensions as a problem-solving tool. As the classroom teacher challenges students to produce a variety of ideas through concept mapping, the gifted education teacher scouts for students who demonstrate high potential in creative thinking related to a real-world issue. The lesson might proceed in this manner:

1. The classroom teacher challenges students to brainstorm solutions to address the problem of deforestation due to the increased demand for nonreusable paper products, and students independently write down every solution they can think of on a concept map (fluency). The more ideas generated by a student equate to more circles on the concept map. Some potential solutions might include the following: increasing taxes on paper products to discourage use, passing more laws to protect trees, inventing new fertilizers to grow trees faster, raising awareness through educational programs, and creating new, synthetic papers. During this phase, the gifted education teacher is actively scouting for students who are brainstorming many responses.

2. As students develop their concept maps, the classroom teacher continues to challenge the class to create solutions across different categories (flexibility). These might include government regulations, technology, education, and recycling efforts. As the gifted education teacher walks around the room, they note who is providing responses across multiple categories.

3. Once students have completed their maps, the classroom teacher asks students to share their solutions, looking for the most innovative approaches (originality). If students all share similar ideas, then it is quite likely that those solutions have already been tried before, so innovative thinking should be highly encouraged. Depending on the shared responses, the classroom teacher might continue to brainstorm with the class to stretch their thinking even further. During this time, the gifted education teacher continues to collect data on students who are sharing unique solutions.

4. Once the class has exhausted its list of solutions, the most original ideas are identified, and the classroom teacher challenges the students to brainstorm ideas and supports for the selected solutions (elaboration). For example, if a solution was "pass laws to protect trees," elaboration might include: Only allow a percentage of trees to be cut down each month, only allow fast-growing trees to be cut down, and limit the land area that production companies can work on. The more details a solution has, the more elaboration is present. This step is crucial in recognizing which solution has the most viable options and also serves as prewriting to develop a proposal to address the problem. Once the proposals are completed, the gifted education teacher is able to gain more insight into which students demonstrated advanced levels of elaboration in their writing.

Dimensions of Creativity to Activate Background Knowledge. Commonly used to activate students' background knowledge, bell-ringers and brain warm-ups are also opportunities to encourage creative thinking. Particularly easy to integrate into Tango Teaching, coteachers can work together to ask students (individually or in a group) to make a list of key ideas they already know about a topic. Students are first given one minute to brainstorm everything they associate with the given topic of study. Example topics might include: Ancient Rome (social studies), fairy tales (English language arts), weather (science), flight (interdisciplinary unit), negative integers (math), or any other content-related topic. After students do this in groups or individually, the coteachers interchangeably ask students to share their ideas while the teachers list them on the board. The teachers then mark out responses that were mentioned by more than one group, leaving only the most "original" responses. At this time, the coteachers may bring attention to original ideas by saying things like, "It looks like Group 2 mentioned a couple of ideas that others did not think of."

The teachers continue to work with the class to categorize responses listed on the board, emphasizing that flexibility is the ability to develop a number of varied ideas. Students are then guided to determine how many categories are shown and are asked if any categories were left out. For example, the coteachers might ask, "Did we consider the technology and tools of Ancient Greece?" Throughout this process, the teachers continue to ask students to articulate how they were able to come up with ideas, perhaps through piggybacking off others' ideas, making connections, thinking through multiple perspectives, or generating specific ideas from general ideas (e.g., thinking of specific Greek gods after listing the general idea of "Greek gods").

The ability for students to create a large number of ideas (fluency) reflects their scope of understanding, while the ability for a student to think through various categories, especially categories (flexibility) not otherwise thought of by other students, reflects breadth of understanding. The discussion of students' ideas reveals the background information a student has about the topic and can be useful as the coteachers plan the next steps of differentiated instruction. From here, elaboration could be encouraged by asking students to develop unanswered questions (e.g., what do we still not know about this idea listed?) to be explored through additional research or inquiry.

Helpful Hints

+ Have students brainstorm ideas that they would like to write about in a journal, on a graffiti wall, etc., as a means to encourage creative thinking. From the fluency of ideas generated, students could continue to expand on a piece of writing with flexibility, originality, and elaboration.

+ Identify specific skills to develop each component of fluency, flexibility, originality, and elaboration. For example, as previously mentioned, students can be encouraged to develop fluency and flexibility by thinking through a number of perspectives and categories and moving from general to specific (and specific to general) ideas. Originality is cultivated through the use of combining ideas, thinking through other perspectives, or adapting an idea to another context. Elaboration is enhanced by teaching skills of visualization and imagery. Refer to the use of SCAMPER in this chapter as an additional strategy to further develop flexibility and originality.

+ Incorporate the four dimensions into academic content, not isolated activities. For example, asking students to list a number of ways a paperclip can be adapted for another use to develop fluency is not directly tied to content. Apply the dimensions directly to content as described in the examples provided (e.g., assess background knowledge, build schema of the content, create solutions related to real-world problems in content domains, use in creative writing).

SCAMPER

SCAMPER (Eberle, 2008) is a creative thinking strategy used to help students generate new ideas or improve ideas based off of existing information. The acronym works through a systematic process: Substitute, Combine, Adapt, Modify (Magnify/Minimize), Put to another use, Eliminate, and Reverse/Rearrange. Teachers can ask, "What if we . . . substitute ____ , combine ____ , etc.?" as a way to encourage students to think of ways to think divergently about solutions to problems or improve existing ideas. SCAMPER is easily integrated through coteaching methods and is also helpful in providing varied creative learning tasks through creating alternate endings to books, analyzing new scientific outcomes, or evaluating historical events. Not every element of SCAMPER needs to be applied to tasks or activities. In addition, SCAMPER also incorporates portions of dimensions of creative thinking by encouraging flexibility and originality.

Examples of Practice

SCAMPER in English Language Arts. After students read a short story or novel, students may apply parts of SCAMPER to create an alternative chapter or version of the story by changing literary elements. Only one or two parts of SCAMPER would be needed, and students may enjoy thinking of their own ideas for SCAMPER prompts. Below are both general and specific examples (applied to "Hansel and Gretel") that students might develop or the teacher may suggest.

+ Substitute the setting for another time period or place. (Specific: Substitute the setting in "Hansel and Gretel" to the year 2040.)
+ Combine by adding another character from a different story you know into the dialogue. (Specific: Add Goldilocks as a character in "Hansel and Gretel.")
+ Adapt the story to be from the minor character's point of view. (Specific: Adapt "Hansel and Gretel" to be told from the father's point of view.)
+ Minimize the story's details by telling it in 10 words or fewer. (Specific: Summarize "Hansel and Gretel" in a poem of 10 words or fewer.)
+ Put the role of the antagonist to another use—allow the antagonist to help the protagonist. (Specific: Explain how the story would be different if the Old Lady helped Hansel and Gretel.)
+ Eliminate the role of character dialogue and focus on the character's internal thoughts about the conflict. (Specific: Tell the story only showing the internal dialogue of Gretel.)

+ Rearrange the order of events by incorporating flashbacks as part of character development. (Specific: Begin the story with the children arriving at the candy house and show flashbacks of their time as young children before the beginning of the real story.)

SCAMPER in Math. Instead of having students work multiple problems of the same format, a classroom teacher may work with the gifted education teacher to use SCAMPER to add alternate approaches for problem solving as a way to differentiate the task.

+ Substitute calculating volume versus area or standard measurement versus metric.
+ Combine another operation into the problem.
+ Adapt and find a new way to solve the problem.
+ Modify the problem to be solved with manipulatives.
+ Put the problem to use in a real world-application.
+ Eliminate one of your variables.
+ Reverse the operation to check the problem.

SCAMPER in Science. SCAMPER can be applied to tier scientific experiments with an additional layer of challenge:

+ Substitute. What if we substituted the independent variable for something else? What would be the effect on the dependent variable?
+ Combine. What else could we combine in the experiment to speed up the change?
+ Adapt. How would you adapt the experiment in future research?
+ Minimize/Maximize. What if we decreased the amount of ____ ? How would this impact the results?
+ Put to other use. In what ways might we apply the results of this experiment to real-world contexts?
+ Eliminate. How might we determine the relationship between the independent variable and the dependent variable without a control group?
+ Reverse/rearrange. Does the dependent variable ever influence the independent variable?

SCAMPER in Social Studies. During a coplanning meeting, teaching partners can plan a post-Socratic seminar reflection on reading the Mayflower Compact. Students might use an element of SCAMPER to delve more deeply into its meaning and influence.

+ Substitute the perspective of the document to that of women.
+ Combine part of the Bill of Rights with The Mayflower Compact.
+ Adapt The Mayflower Compact to present-day language.

+ Modify the document to show its meaning in 10 words or fewer.
+ Put to other use. How has this document been "put to another use" through influencing future government documents?
+ Eliminate the word *covenant* from the document and discuss the impact it would have on the overall meaning.
+ Rearrange. The document was a contract in which the settlers consented to follow the compact's rules and regulations for the sake of order and survival. What if the settlers had signed it for the sake of submitting to one authoritarian leader instead of to each other?

Helpful Hints

+ To encourage students' creativity with SCAMPER, create a "Happy SCAMPER" corner. This could be a bulletin board display, scrapbook, museum exhibit, etc., to acknowledge extraordinary SCAMPERing abilities.
+ For students who need extra support with SCAMPER, provide prepared questions to help them work through the process. For students who need a deeper level of challenge, have them create their own questions with the acronym, justify their reasoning in their answers, and provide a context for real-world connection.

Stretch Thinking Prompts

The stretch prompts serve as tools for vertical differentiation, providing opportunities to "stretch" students to engage more deeply with content. The first question on each prompt taps into what students know about the topic. This is followed by questions that extend student thinking into deeper understanding or transference of knowledge into other contexts (see Resource 8: Stretch Prompts). These prompts are designed with built-in tiers of support for extended learning, strategic thinking, and reasoning.

Once students are familiar with the stretch prompts, these could be cut into strips (even laminated) and put into envelopes to distribute to groups of students, ready to be used as discussion starters during think-pair-share moments of the lesson, exit tickets for formative assessment, or class openers to review content from the day before (and extend it). If used as a formative assessment, the teacher may ask students to respond in writing to a prompt on their own paper. For collaborative group learning, these prompts can be used simply to provide a focus for small-group

RESOURCE 8
Stretch Prompts

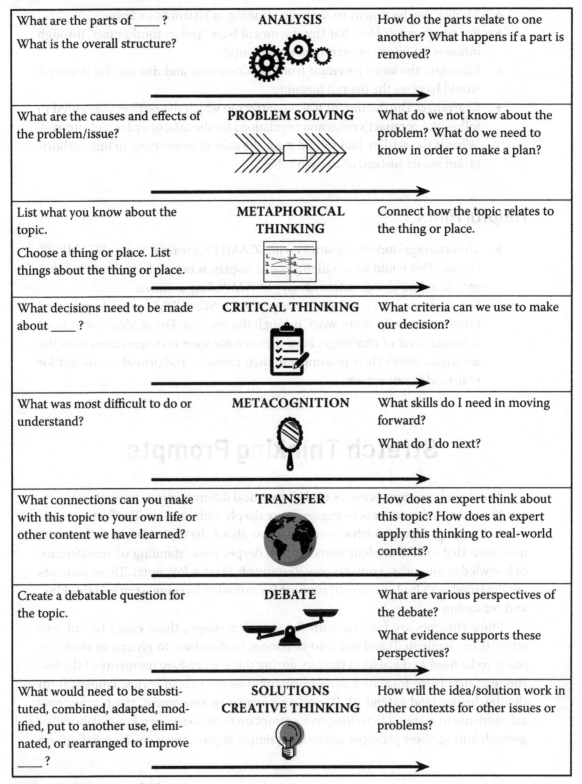

What are the parts of ____? What is the overall structure?	**ANALYSIS**	How do the parts relate to one another? What happens if a part is removed?
What are the causes and effects of the problem/issue?	**PROBLEM SOLVING**	What do we not know about the problem? What do we need to know in order to make a plan?
List what you know about the topic. Choose a thing or place. List things about the thing or place.	**METAPHORICAL THINKING**	Connect how the topic relates to the thing or place.
What decisions need to be made about ____?	**CRITICAL THINKING**	What criteria can we use to make our decision?
What was most difficult to do or understand?	**METACOGNITION**	What skills do I need in moving forward? What do I do next?
What connections can you make with this topic to your own life or other content we have learned?	**TRANSFER**	How does an expert think about this topic? How does an expert apply this thinking to real-world contexts?
Create a debatable question for the topic.	**DEBATE**	What are various perspectives of the debate? What evidence supports these perspectives?
What would need to be substituted, combined, adapted, modified, put to another use, eliminated, or rearranged to improve ____?	**SOLUTIONS CREATIVE THINKING**	How will the idea/solution work in other contexts for other issues or problems?

Note. Created by E. Mofield.

Collaboration, Coteaching, and Coaching in Gifted Education © Prufrock Press Inc.

discussions in which students respond in interactive notebooks, gallery walks, chart paper, or group notes.

These prompts can also serve as a simple planning tool for the teacher to refer to as ways to stretch student thinking during any part of a lesson. A key to using these prompts is knowing how to apply them to the lesson content. Teachers cannot simply copy these prompts and distribute them to students as a worksheet without intentionally guiding students to focus on an aspect of the lesson. The prompts need to be thoughtfully embedded and adapted to content.

In Chapter 10, these prompts are also presented with sentence frames (see p. 176), which can support students in developing written or oral responses to these prompts, especially for younger students or ELLs. These are not necessarily meant to be worksheets, but rather simple discussion or writing prompts for eliciting deeper thinking.

Examples of Practice

Think-Pair-Share Discussion. When coplanning ways for students to reflect and apply deeper levels of understanding to content, consider using 4–5 stretch prompts for student-to-student discussion. For example, in a lesson on the Industrial Revolution, the teachers may decide to use the analysis, problem-solving, critical thinking, and debate prompt to be placed in envelopes for each pair (you may also consider laminating these). Students select one card and discuss it with a partner. The teacher may need to be ready with specific ways the questions apply to the content to guide the students' thinking. For example, for the analysis prompt, students might be asked "What are the major ideas, people, and events that make up the Industrial Revolution?" or "How did these ideas, events, and/or people influence each other?" Debate prompts might include "Did change lead to progress?" and "What are two perspectives, and what evidence supports this?" With the debate prompt, students can also identify the debate or controversy on their own as a way to reflect on lesson content during small group discussion. Students might record their discussion responses in group notes to be turned in for formative assessment. As demonstrated in these examples, the prompts can be adapted to fit the context of the topic.

Synthesizing Content Using Metaphorical Stretch Thinking. As two teaching partners plan a lesson on interpreting poetry, they might choose to use the prompt for metaphorical thinking to incorporate as part of Tier Teaching. At the end of a unit on literary elements in poetry, the classroom teacher plans to work with students on using the elements in a review game, while the gifted education teacher plans to work with students using the metaphorical stretch thinking prompt. Students list specific literary elements used to interpret poetry (sound devices, rhythm, tone, structure, rhyme, symbolism, etc.) on the left side while briefly reviewing the meaning of the terms. Then, the gifted education teacher asks students to list features of a thing or place on the right side of the chart. For example, using an amusement park, students might list roller coaster rides, fast passes, cotton candy, carousels, souvenir T-shirts, etc. Students then draw arrows across the chart to explain how a literary element is like a feature of an amusement park: The lack of punctuation (structure) is an acceptable way to "break the rules" of grammar to convey meaning, just as a fast pass is an acceptable way to "break rules" to experience something meaningful at the amusement park.

Helpful Hints

+ Be prepared to help students apply the prompt to the content. Have a debatable question or problem/issue ready for them to identify and discuss (as it relates to the prompt).
+ Know that all prompts may not be as applicable to specific content and topics. Preplan which ones might be used during the lesson.
+ It is not necessary for students to always provide written responses to prompts. These serve as excellent discussion starters, so you may consider building in structures for student accountable talk.
+ These prompts are excellent sources of questioning during Stretch and Scout Teaching, providing additional opportunities for more in-depth exploration of content.

Putting It All Together

Although this chapter has addressed strategies that are easily adapted into existing lessons, these strategies, in many cases, are also easily integrated with one another. For example, Kaplan's (2009) depth and complexity thinking tools or de Bono's (1985/2016) Six Thinking Hats could easily be integrated into the double fishbone as a means to think more holistically about the problem or issue. In short, we encourage you to think flexibly about how these strategies can be implemented with advanced content and in conjunction with other strategies.

Chapter 7

Strategies for Deeper Inquiry

Beyond adding additional tiers and layers of depth and complexity to lessons, sometimes coplanning involves a more integrated approach to instructional design from the onset. For example, this might include considering multiple standards, examining flexible grouping options through preassessment data, creating essential guiding questions, and developing synthesis tasks in ways that allow for students to dive into deeper levels of inquiry. As such, these strategies require more in-depth collaboration and offer gifted students opportunities for sustained cognitive engagement with advanced content.

The following strategies are adaptable to a variety of grade levels and content areas and are easily incorporated through coteaching. The strategies shared throughout this chapter continue to recognize the importance of the classroom teacher contributing to the coplanning process as the content specialist, while the gifted education teacher shares various strategies that lead students to deeper levels of conceptual understanding. As collaborative partnerships continue to develop through the TEAM frame (trust, engage, align, maintain), the scope of coplanning broadens. As you consider the following strategies, continue to think through how they might be implemented within your own classroom teaching or small-group work, as these self-reflective experiences provide opportunities to collaborate with others in more authentic ways.

Concept Attainment

Concept attainment (Bruner, 1973) provides students with an opportunity to use critical thinking to understand the essential attributes of a concept. This strategy is most successful in introducing concepts with clear critical characteristics. Once the concept has been chosen, students are provided with examples of keywords and phrases that align with the concept and keywords and phrases that do not. The teacher then categorizes these keywords and phrases into the appropriate "yes" and "no" categories. As students see the categories develop, they begin to formulate their rationale for what they believe the overarching concept could be. Through ongoing clues, students continue to test and refine their rationales. Once the concept has been confirmed, students reflect upon the concept attainment process and demonstrate their level of understanding through a synthesis task. As a formative assessment measure, concept attainment also provides insight into students' readiness levels, serving as a guide for continued differentiation throughout the remainder of the unit.

Examples of Practice

Science Cluster Group. While waiting for a faculty meeting to begin, a second-grade teacher begins to talk about her upcoming unit on natural resources. She has already designated the learning standards and instructional goals, but she is concerned that the current delivery method is not going to engage her gifted cluster group. She schedules a time to brainstorm with the gifted education teacher on how to introduce the material to this group of students in a different manner. During the brainstorming session, the gifted education teacher suggests the concept attainment strategy, and after further discussion, they begin coplanning through this instructional approach.

As the lesson is developed, the classroom teacher's content-area expertise is invaluable as they identify the critical attributes needed to introduce the concept of natural resources to the class. From these critical attributes, a list of "yes" examples and "no" examples is created to build students' conceptual understanding. For this lesson, the teachers' generated list might include the following examples and nonexamples:

+ **"Yes" examples of natural resources:** water, air, coal, oil, iron, soil, timber
+ **"No" examples of natural resources:** plastic, smog, chocolate, lemonade, gasoline, paper, concrete

Once the list is generated, the lesson is ready to be introduced to students. Together, the two teachers decide that the gifted education teacher will model the lesson for the classroom teacher to observe and take notes (see Resource 5, p. 68).

At the onset of the lesson, the gifted education teacher tells the students that they are going to be provided with "yes" and "no" clues related to the unit, but the teacher is not going to tell the students what the unit is going to be about. That is the students' job to determine. The teacher describes the unit to the students as a riddle that they need to solve. The students are excited and ready for the challenge. To help monitor their thinking, students use graphic organizers to write each provided clue in the appropriate "yes" or "no" column as it is presented. This same graphic organizer includes a section for students to formulate their ongoing and evolving rationale for the concept of study (see Resource 9: Concept Attainment Clues). The gifted education teacher provides one "yes" clue and one "no" clue at a time. After writing the two clues on the handout, students write down ideas about what they believe the concept might be, as they try to solve the "riddle." Table 17 provides an example of how a student might work through this exercise.

As the process evolves, students constantly adjust their thinking until they identify the concept. As a result, students develop a deeper conceptual understanding of content.

Once the process is complete and the topic of natural resources has been discovered, students are asked to reflect on how their thinking evolved throughout the process, at what point they were certain of the concept, and how this process helped develop a deeper understanding of the unit of study. This could be accomplished through independent journals, think-pair-share, or classroom discussions. To further assess student learning, students might be asked to generate a list of natural resources used in making their school supplies or natural resources found in the classroom.

Upon completion of the lesson, the gifted education teacher and classroom teacher schedule a time to discuss the lesson and any insights, questions, or takeaways that the classroom teacher had after observing the lesson. Further collaboration could focus on next steps within this particular unit or how to implement the concept attainment strategy in future units.

Concept Game. After actively observing the concept attainment model lesson on natural resources and reflecting on the modeled lesson with the gifted education teacher, the classroom teacher decides to play a concept attainment game to help their students reinforce classifications in one of their language arts lessons. The teacher does this by playing the game of Sally's Favorite Things. In this game, the classroom teacher chooses a concept that "Sally" loves and one that she does not. In the example that follows, Sally loves common nouns, but she does not love proper nouns. The classroom teacher begins by making a statement that accurately represents the two categories. Students then take turns providing statements to deter-

RESOURCE 9
Concept Attainment Clues

Directions: Write the "yes" and "no" examples in the boxes below. Then write your ideas about what you think the concept might be under "My Thinking."

Examples (Yes)	Examples (No)	My Thinking

TABLE 17
Student Responses for Concept Attainment Strategy

Examples (Yes)	Examples (No)	My Thinking
air	paper	things that are made of matter but you can't see
water	concrete	matter that a human body can breathe, drink, or eat
soil	chocolate	things that are needed to grow a plant

mine what concept Sally loves versus the concept that she does not. The teacher responds to each student's statement, providing further clues for the rule. As the game continues, students listen carefully to the clues to determine the overarching rule. The game might proceed in this manner:

+ **Teacher:** Sally loves amusement parks but does not love Disney World.
+ **Student 1:** Sally loves ice cream but does not love football.
+ **Teacher's response to Student 1:** Sally loves them both.
+ **Student 2:** Sally loves Mars but does not love planets.
+ **Teacher's response to Student 2:** Sally loves planets but does not love Mars.
+ **Student 3:** Sally loves Little Miss Muffet but does not love Humpty Dumpty.
+ **Teacher's response to Student 3:** Sally does not love either of them.
+ **Student 4:** Sally loves boats but does not love the Titanic.
+ **Teacher's response to Student 4:** Correct! (Teacher then proceeds with another example.) Sally loves her sister but does not love Sally.

The classroom teacher stresses that as students solve the rule of the game, they do not say the rule aloud, instead they continue to provide examples when it is their turn. This not only provides further clues to the remaining students, but also helps the classroom teacher assess concept mastery for each student. Further, as students test their statements, it encourages fluency of ideas, as part of the dimensions of creative thinking strategy. The game continues until all students are able to make correct statements that align with the rule. For students who have difficulty with working memory, consider allowing them to create a written list of shared answers.

Concept Development Model

The Concept Development Model (Taba et al., 1971) allows students to see the "big picture" of what they are learning by developing and supporting broad generalizations, rules, or predictions about the content. The steps of this model are as follows:

1. Present students with a list of keywords, items, equations, phrases, etc., associated with a topic at the beginning of a unit of study.
2. Ask students to sort and categorize the words and then label the categories. Students should justify and explain why these words belong in these categories. (*Hint*: Ask students not to have an "other" category.)
3. Ask students to regroup the words again, forming different categories. Ask students to explain their reasoning behind the new organization.
4. By using their descriptive labels (in step 4 and 5), students generate predictions, hypotheses, rules, and/or content-specific generalizations.
5. Throughout the remainder of the unit, students collect evidence to support or refute their previously created predictions, hypotheses, or generalizations that were generated at the beginning of the unit.

Throughout the process, students should be encouraged to be flexible in their thinking, allowing for words to be categorized in multiple categories when appropriate.

Examples of Practice

Social Studies Sort. A middle school social studies teacher schedules a time to collaborate with the gifted education teacher with the purpose of adding an additional level of complexity and critical thinking to an upcoming unit on the 13 original American colonies. The classroom teacher comes prepared to the meeting, with an understanding of shared responsibility, and communicates the learning objectives and instructional standards for the unit. Because of their strong collaborative relationship with the gifted education teacher, the social studies teacher reaches out to seek varied approaches to engaging students with the content. Together, the two teachers decide to coplan a lesson using the concept development model.

Upon sharing the nonfiction resources they were planning to incorporate in this unit, the classroom teacher and gifted education teacher collaboratively begin to select keywords and phrases found throughout the varying texts related to the 13 colonies. Table 18 provides an example of keywords the teachers might identify.

These words are then presented to the students at the onset of the unit to sort and categorize into meaningful groups. Then, students label the groups. Samples of student-generated categories, labels, and associated responses might include:

+ **Sources of food:** fishing, hunting, farming
+ **Desirable outcomes:** growth, power, expansion, freedom, opportunity, profit, land, safety, trade
+ **Causes for war:** control, competition, religion, persecution, taxes, disputes

TABLE 18

Keywords for 13 Original Colonies Concept Development

Control	Settlers	Religion	Natives	Founded	Safety
Disease	Growth	Power	Opportunity	Profit	Land
Trade	Disputes	Competition	Expansion	Persecution	Farming
Taxes	Hunting	Freedom	Fishing	Harsh Winters	Natural Resources

As students work either independently or in groups during this portion of the lesson, the classroom teacher rotates around the room asking students to justify their groupings by explaining how and why specific words belong in the categories. If implemented during Scout and Stretch teaching, this would be an opportunity to recognize and continue to challenge advanced-level students even further (see Helpful Hints section).

Next, the teacher would ask students to regroup the words again by asking, "How might we group these differently? Would some of these words belong in more than one group?" (e.g., power and expansion may also belong in causes for war). Students may develop new groupings, such as:

+ **Economics/goods:** taxes, fishing, farming, hunting, profit, trade
+ **Geographic/political:** expansion, power, growth, disputes, land, safety
+ **Cultural/social:** religion, freedom, opportunities

Once students create and justify their regroupings, they use their descriptive labels to create predictions, hypotheses, rules, or generalizations about the original 13 colonies. These statements can be based on either the first or second groupings. Sample statements might include:

+ Settlers left negative circumstances in pursuit of positive ones (generalization).
+ The 13 colonies provided new economic opportunities and freedoms (generalization).
+ Although desirable outcomes motivated early settlers to come to America, upon arrival, many wished they had never left England (prediction).

Students write their generated statements on a graphic organizer that allows them to provide support for or against their statements (see Resource 10: Testing My Predictions). This graphic organizer provides students with a place to record information throughout the unit to either confirm or disprove their thinking produced in this activity.

RESOURCE 10
Testing My Predictions

Directions: Using your list and categories, write a prediction, hypothesis, rule, or generalization in each section of the first column. As you learn new information, write evidence that provides support for or against what is written in the first column.

My Prediction, Hypothesis, Rule, or Generalization	Support For	Support Against

Helpful Hints

As students work either independently or with groups to sort, categorize, and label key concepts, some students will inevitably complete the task before others. These are learning behaviors that should be noted during Scout Teaching. In continuing with Stretch Teaching, present these students with Challenge Cards once they have labeled all of their categories. This is a great way to not only continue to challenge groups who might finish early, but also continue to encourage dimensions of creativity (see Chapter 6) through fluency, flexibility, and originality.

Challenge Cards suggestions might include:

+ Add three new words or phrases to two of your already established categories.
+ Choose four of the following universal themes to add to your already established categories: power, exploration, change, systems, order versus chaos, conflict.
+ Create a more descriptive label for two of your categories.
+ Identify three words that could potentially be placed in a different category and explain why.

Metaphorical Expression

Metaphorical expression opens the door for high-achieving and gifted learners to make abstract connections to classroom content. Metaphor, in its literal sense, means the transference of ideas from one set of concepts to an unrelated set of different concepts. In the context of classroom learning, this strategy presents students with an opportunity to activate knowledge to delve deeper into the conceptual understanding of a unit of study.

Examples of Practice

Metaphorical Math Properties. A third-grade teacher collaborates with the gifted education teacher on a unit to teach the math properties of operations. The third-grade teacher anticipates that their gifted and high-achieving students will master the properties with few repetitions, but from past experience, they realize that the remainder of their students will probably need continued support and extra practice with this concept. The classroom teacher proactively schedules a meeting with the gifted education teacher to address this need for differentiation.

As the two teachers begin collaborating on this lesson, the classroom teacher describes their gifted learners as highly creative. The classroom teacher is especially interested in learning how to create an opportunity for their high-ability math students to approach this unit in a manner that will play to their strengths. Through the collaborative process, the teachers decide to use the coteaching model of Tier Teaching. The classroom teacher will lead one group through direct instruction and gradual release, and the gifted education teacher will lead the advanced group by introducing the concepts and leading the students to create metaphorical expressions of the multiplication properties.

After ensuring that the advanced group has an understanding of metaphors, the students are tasked with creating metaphors that represent the multiplication properties. Table 19 provides possible student-generated examples that emerge from this lesson.

As the students create their own metaphorical expressions to demonstrate their understanding of these concepts, they are also given the opportunity to create visual representations to share with the class and display in the classroom, helping to solidify the concepts for all learners.

Metaphorical Geology. During a sixth-grade PLC in which the gifted education teacher is in attendance to offer any additional insight or support, the science teacher shares how they will be teaching the different types of rocks in their next unit of study. The science teacher is trying to branch out from relying solely on the science textbook, and although they feel confident that the text describes the different attributes of igneous, sedimentary, and metamorphic rocks in a well-written manner, the science teacher also recognizes that it is not engaging students in learning. The science teacher also shares that they have been having some discipline issues with some of their gifted students and asks to brainstorm solutions to address both of these issues. After scheduling a meeting to discuss this and learning more about the classroom teacher's desired outcomes, the gifted education teacher shares the metaphorical expression strategy with the teacher. Together, they coplan a lesson to incorporate the metaphorical thinking strategy with science content, and although coteaching is not an option with the teachers' schedules, the classroom teacher is equipped to use the strategy.

Instead of working directly from the textbook, students are given the opportunity to demonstrate their understanding of the different types of rock by creating a rock band's promotional poster. In addition to the typical touring dates, the main focus of the poster is to describe and illustrate how each member of the band is a metaphorical expression of one of the three types of rocks. After seeing the displayed rock band posters and reading the band members' bios, it was evident that students had a clear conceptual understanding of the differences between the different types of rocks and how they were formed. One poster promoted The Pounding Heads' epic rock concert being held at Stonehenge:

TABLE 19

Possible Student-Generated Responses for Metaphorical Expression

Mathematical Property	Student-Generated Metaphorical Expressions
Identity Property of Multiplication: $5 \times 1 = 5$	The identity property is a mirror: A person looks in a mirror and always sees their own identity looking back.
Commutative Property of Multiplication: $2 \times 3 = 3 \times 2$	The commutative property is a commute: A dad commutes to work by driving his car to the office and back home again, driving the same route between locations each day.
Associative Property of Multiplication: $(7 \times 8) \times 9 = 7 \times (8 \times 9)$	The associative property is the buddy system: Two classmates are buddy reading together while another classmate reads independently. Then one of the buddy readers decides to read alone, so the other classmate joins the previous independent reader to buddy read together. The switching of who is associated with buddy reading does not change the fact that they are all reading.
Distributive Property of Multiplication: $2(4 + 6) = 2 \times 4 + 2 \times 6$	The distributive property is making friends: A new student joined the classroom and at first does not know anybody but soon wants to equally distribute their friendship to the others in the classroom.

+ The lead singer, Slash Sedimentary, was known for his many layers being expressed through song. Despite his complex vocals, Slash was quite the "softy" off the stage and had been caught crumbling to pieces while out in public.
+ Max Metamorphic, the band's drummer, was known for his amazing ability on the drums. He played with extreme pressure, often creating heat from his intensity.
+ Finally, there was Iggy Igneous, the band's lead guitarist. Iggy's cool hardened appearance set him apart from his bandmates, and although he often erupted with a quick temper, he would quickly cool down. His glassy eyes made girls swoon.

Helpful Hints

+ Present students with a "grab bag" of random items (rubber ducky, sunglasses, pen, action figure, sponge, etc.). The more random the items, the more engaging the experience. Students select an item from the grab bag and metaphorically connect that item to the unit of study. For example, in learning about photosynthesis, a student might pull the sponge from the bag and say that the sponge absorbs water much like a plant absorbs sunlight to harness energy during the process of photosynthesis.

+ Combine metaphorical expression with concept development. In the previous mathematical properties scenario, provide students with multiple examples of the different properties without any explanation. Have the students first sort the equations into categories and then label the categories before providing them with the official names of the properties.

Mystery Box

The mystery strategy builds on gifted learners' natural curiosity, intrigue, and desire to engage through the power of inquiry. Lessons that use this approach begin by presenting students with riddles or representative artifacts that must be solved in order to move forward in a unit of study. Students continue to work through this inquiry process to learn key concepts and objectives, and in doing so, develop content-specific generalizations. This strategy provides gifted learners an opportunity to explore advanced content through abstract and higher level thinking.

Examples of Practice

Time Capsule Mystery. While coplanning a unit on the Progressive Era, the classroom teacher shares the state standards and the unit's guiding question: "Why is the period from 1880 to 1917 known as the Progressive Era?" with the gifted education teacher. In addition, the classroom teacher also shares the key terms, people, and events that students are responsible for learning by reading primary and secondary sources. Likewise, the gifted education teacher shares their knowledge of gifted strategies, and together, the two teachers decide that the mystery box strategy would work well for this unit.

The teachers work together to create a time capsule filled with riddle-type artifacts that represent the essential learnings from the unit of study. To do this, the key terms, people, and events are used to create a list of items that could be represented in the time capsule (e.g., Theodore Roosevelt, Henry Ford, the Triangle Shirtwaist Factory, immigration, muckrakers, etc.). Once the list is created, the two teachers work to brainstorm a list of easily found and accessible items that could represent each of the items on the list. Table 20 provides potential time capsule artifacts that might be used.

The two teachers try to find three-dimensional items for all of the artifacts, but they also use several printed pictures and primary sources for some of the more obscure items. Once the teachers decide how these match to the corresponding key terms, people, and events, the representative artifacts are placed in a "mystery box" that students will open as a time capsule.

Before the time capsule is introduced to the class, the classroom teacher and gifted education teacher find additional resources to use as reference materials for the time capsule artifacts. These include primary sources and secondary sources pulled from the school library, the local public library, classroom collections, and other various sources. These will be made readily available to the students once the time capsule has been opened.

On the day the time capsule is introduced to the students, the guiding question "Why is the period from 1880 to 1917 known as the Progressive Era?" is also introduced. In knowing the time period, the students become perplexed when such unusual items are found in the time capsule, and their curiosity is activated. Each student is tasked with selecting one artifact and using effective questioning and search techniques to identify what key term, person, or event it represents. The students proceed to answer the guiding question as follows:

1. With only knowing the time period, students generate searchable words associated with their artifact to help them identify what their artifact represents. For example, if the student selected the triangle piece of T-shirt material, they might include the known dates of the Progressive Era with the keywords *triangle*, *material*, *cotton*, *T-shirt*, etc., into a list of "search words."

2. Students use these search words as a guide while using the various reference sources (e.g., computers, primary sources, textbooks, trade books) to identify their represented item.

3. Students also ask the classroom teacher "yes" or "no" questions to narrow down their search based on their research so far. In doing so, this valuable information continues to guide their inquiry. For example, after doing some preliminary research to identify the relevance of the teddy bear, a student might let the teacher know that the textile industry experienced a great deal of growth during this time period. The student also shares that the teddy bear was named after Theodore Roosevelt. With this information, the student would like to know which direction the research should continue, so the student might ask, "Does the teddy bear have a stronger representation to a particular person versus the textile it is made out of?" In this case, the teacher would answer "yes," providing the student with information to help narrow the focus toward Theodore Roosevelt and away from the expanding textile industry.

TABLE 20
Potential Time Capsule Artifacts for Progressive Era Mystery Box

Key Term, Person, or Event	Representative Artifact
Henry Ford	Toy car
The Triangle Shirtwaist Factory	A triangle piece of material cut from an old T-shirt
Theodore Roosevelt	Teddy bear
Immigration	A small model of the Statue of Liberty
Muckrakers	Cleaned meat label packaging on a hand rake

4. Through this ongoing process, students identify what their artifact represents and then continue with researching to learn more about the relevance of the key term, person, or event to the Progressive Era.

5. Once research is concluded, students present their findings to the class.

6. After classroom presentations, the students have an understanding of why all of the artifacts are representative of the Progressive Era. They then work to create content-specific generalizations about the time period. For example, from learning about Mother Jones, The Triangle Shirtwaist Factory fire, and the muckrakers, students might conclude, "Horrible working conditions were a common occurrence during the Progressive Era." By joining this conclusion together with understanding the advancements that were made during this period of history, the following generalization might be created: "Progress requires sacrifice."

After the students continue to develop more generalizations, they would integrate them into answering the guiding question from the unit. In terms of this generalization, the student response might include irony, as students would begin to recognize that although the Progressive Era was named for the multitude of advancements, there were also many sacrifices made to propel the United States forward in technology during that time.

Hero's Journey Through Mystery. After successfully coteaching with the gifted education teacher, a classroom teacher is excited to coplan the next lesson, which is focused on students applying what they have already learned about the hero's journey through literature. Together, the classroom teacher and gifted education teacher develop stations to incorporate during Carousel Teaching, when gifted learners will be able to work through various stations that have been vertically differentiated to meet the level of rigor needed for sustained inquiry and critical thinking.

In this case, the classroom teacher and gifted education teacher create one station where a variety of children's picture books are made available (e.g., *The Little Mermaid, Last Stop on Market Street, Where the Wild Things Are, The Lion King,* etc.) for students to independently work through to identify the various attributes of the hero's journey (e.g., hero, call to adventure, mentor, helper, threshold guardian, abyss, etc.). At a different station, the classroom teacher works with students who need additional guidance and leads them through a structured activity to identify how the hero's journey was symbolized in the Harry Potter series.

At the vertical differentiated station, the gifted education teacher works with advanced learners to have them synthesize what they have learned about the hero's journey into a prediction of what the next class novel will be about, but they will not be told the title of the novel. Instead, they are given a mystery box of items including a temporary tattoo, a piece of fur, a plastic cow, a whale bath toy, and other items signifying important storyline components of the upcoming novel (*The House of the Scorpion*).

The gifted education teacher works to stretch students' creativity as they write a prediction on a graphic organizer for the upcoming novel, including all aspects of the hero's journey in conjunction with all of the mystery box items. The only hint students are given is that the book deals with cloning, and that must be part of their hero's journey predicted storyline. Later, as the novel is read, students identify what the items truly represent in the novel as well as their significance and role in the main character's hero's journey.

Helpful Hints

+ Use as an introduction to a unit by providing just a few primary sources, key vocabulary, character traits, equations, or key phrases at the beginning of a unit and ask students to formulate a hypothesis about the upcoming unit of study based off the provided information. As the unit progresses, students can continue to gather information to confirm or refute their hypotheses as to what the items represent.
+ Have students create their own mystery boxes for independent study topics or other units of study.

Other Inquiry Approaches

Problem-based learning is beyond the scope of this text, but collaborators can certainly consider the value of creating an ill-structured problem for students to grapple with throughout a unit of study. Together, teachers can find or develop problem scenarios that set the stage for Creative Problem Solving (Treffinger & Isaksen, 2005). This involves understanding ideas (exploring and framing problems), generating solution ideas, and preparing action plans for carrying out a solution. Together, the classroom teacher and gifted education teacher may work to develop or find possible scenarios related to the content that would require sustained inquiry and use of multiple sources over a period of time.

For example, a science teacher and gifted education teacher may work together to plan a unit around environmental science. They search to find a few articles around the disappearing honeybee population and causes of colony collapse disorder. After students read articles, the teachers may situate the task into a scenario such as the following:

> Because you and your team are renown experts in environmental science, you have been selected to work with the Global Environmental Agency to analyze the issues around the global decline of the honeybee population. Now that you have reviewed the information packet (the articles), clarify the problem, create possible solution ideas, and develop a formal plan for action to present before the GEA.

Problem scenarios also can set the stage for using many of the strategies suggested in Chapter 6. For example, students may think critically about the issue or problem using the elements of reasoning and unravel "the mess" of the problem by using the double fishbone. Solutions can be created using dimensions of creativity and SCAMPER.

High-Quality Gifted Curriculum Units

As teachers work together to coplan and codesign lesson experiences, they may consider the many high-quality curriculum materials available through various publishers. The NAGC Curriculum Network has established criteria for what constitutes high-quality curriculum. A number of curricular units have been recognized for meeting or exceeding these standards and can be found at https://www.nagc.org/curriculum-awards. Teachers may consider using these resources as they coplan instruction for gifted learners. Some of the units might be shared with classroom teachers to be taught in entirety to an advanced class, or perhaps parts of the unit are used for various stations in Carousel Teaching or Safari Teaching. Other considerations include choosing specific reading passages, models, or activities from these units to supplement a teacher's planned delivery of content.

Some of these evidence-supported units have been developed by universities in collaboration with educators:

+ Vanderbilt Programs for Talented Youth's curriculum series for gifted and advanced learners (Prufrock Press),
+ William & Mary's gifted curriculum units (Kendall Hunt Publishing and Prufrock Press),
+ University of Virginia's CLEAR curriculum units (Prufrock Press),
+ University of Connecticut's M^3 math units (Kendall Hunt Publishing),
+ Shelagh Gallagher and other authors' problem-based learning units (Royal Fireworks Press), and
+ the Jacob's Ladder Reading Comprehension Program (Prufrock Press).

Resources like these, developed with the gifted learner in mind, are often great places to start in coplanning for long-term ongoing collaborative instruction.

Chapter 8

Instructional Coaching in Gifted Education

Instructional coaching is about building capacity in other teachers to improve practices, refine skills, and encounter new possibilities in their teaching. The role of a coach involves thinking with teachers in guiding them to recognize their own strengths and solve their own problems and challenges. As its etymological definition denotes, the word *coach* elicits an image of a carriage as a means of travel, focused on movement. The word conveys the idea of guiding an individual to move to where they desire to be. Coaching ultimately focuses on future growth in instructional practice. A coach, therefore, is not a tool for "fixing" people, nor a police officer enforcing rules for the administration (Aguilar, 2013), but a "cothinking partner" who facilitates change within an individual through providing contexts for self-reflection and growth.

In a collaborative role as a gifted education teacher, it may be easy to step in to solve problems for a fellow peer (e.g., develop challenging assignments, combat underachievement, or address a behavior issue in a gifted student). Collaboration through coaching, however, involves more intentional listening and understanding a teacher's concerns and self-selected goals. Rather than offering direct advice to a teacher, coaching involves navigating solutions to problems with the teacher through providing structures for learning (e.g., modeling, observing, conferencing) and reflective feedback. In the context of this chapter, we refer to the coaching relationship as one between the coach (who may be a gifted education teacher, coordinator, or instructional coach) and another educator (e.g., specialist, classroom teacher, other gifted education teacher).

Like other collaboration models used throughout this book, coaching can serve as a vehicle for professional learning to help others grow and improve in their practices around serving and teaching gifted students. Coaching directly supports the evidence-based practices tied to the NAGC (2019) Gifted Programming Standards, especially the following:

> 6.4.2. Educators participate in professional learning that is sustained over time, incorporates collaboration and reflection, is goal-aligned and data-driven, is coherent, embedded and transferable, includes regular follow-up, and seeks evidence of positive impact on teacher practice and on increased student learning.

While exploring the coaching models and methods within this chapter, notice the emphasis on how reflection around a teacher's own selected goals drives the learning within the coaching process. We continue to emphasize the use of the Collaborative Process Model: Set a purpose, plan, and reflect. This is applied to effective coaching practices within the Collaborative Process Model Coaching Tool (Resource 11, p. 137) and will be explained throughout the chapter.

Coaching Models

There are a number of coaching models in education: cognitive coaching, instructional coaching, peer coaching, and many others. Determining which model to use should be guided by your purpose in implementing coaching practices, your role, and your context. Cognitive coaching focuses on reflecting on the thinking behind behaviors and practices. It involves uncovering awareness of thinking through self-evaluation, self-reflection, and self-direction (Costa & Gamston, 2015; Kee et al., 2010). Instructional coaching focuses on the teacher self-selecting a goal, followed by developing specific skills related to this goal through reading, seeing the strategy modeled, or practicing the strategy (DeWitt, 2017). Another form of coaching, often referred to in gifted education contexts, is peer coaching (Cotabish & Robinson, 2012; Fogarty & Tschida, 2018; Tieso, 2004). Peer coaching is "a confidential process through which two or more professional colleagues work together to reflect on current practices; expand, refine, and build new skills; share ideas; teach one another; conduct classroom research; or solve problems in the workplace" (Robbins, 1991, p. 1). Coteaching pairs well with peer coaching, as the classroom teacher learns and refines new practices from coteaching with the gifted education teacher (Fogarty & Tschida, 2018). Although the approaches are somewhat different, the models can certainly apply and even blend with one another in contexts aimed to improve pedagogy related to educating gifted students.

Throughout this chapter, we mainly refer to coaching as instructional coaching, although components of cognitive and peer coaching are embedded as well. Here we share two instructional coaching models that can be adapted for the purpose of coaching for building capacity among individuals teaching gifted students: (1) the Coaching Continuum Model (Norwood & Burke, 2011) and (2) Content Coaching (West, 2009).

The Coaching Continuum Model

The Coaching Continuum Model (Norwood & Burke, 2011) involves a gradual release of responsibility consisting of four phases. This moves from the classroom teacher observing what and how a strategy works to the classroom teacher's independent implementation of the strategy or practice.

+ **Phase 1:** Modeling of a strategy. Here, the gifted education teacher (serving in the role of a coach) might use demonstration teaching to model ways to vertically differentiate instruction for gifted learners or guide students through deeper levels of inquiry (see Chapters 6 and 7). Resource 5: Observing Instructional Strategies for Gifted Learners (p. 68) is recommended to use when a strategy is modeled to allow for reflection of how the teacher might use the strategy in the future.

+ **Phase 2:** Collaborative activities. This phase involves the heart of the planning process within the Collaborative Process Model. Together, shared decisions are made relating to teaching, planning, problem solving, curriculum development, and student data. This may include many of the processes discussed in Chapter 3. This phase builds capacity as both teachers together serve as thinking partners to coplan instruction.

+ **Phase 3:** Independent implementation of the lesson. The classroom teacher and gifted education teacher/coach meet during a preconference to discuss how the classroom teacher plans to deliver a lesson and include specific strategies to use with gifted learners. The classroom teacher then teaches the lesson while the coach observes. This is then followed by a conference reflecting on what worked, what did not work, and next steps in instruction.

+ **Phase 4:** Celebrate. Both the classroom teacher and coach celebrate the gradual release of responsibility, acknowledging the professional growth made throughout the process.

The Content Coaching Model

The Content Coaching Model (West, 2009) aims to develop teachers' habits of reasoning associated with a specific content discipline so that these "ways of thinking" can be cultivated within students. For example, a classroom teacher can focus on developing reasoning, critical thinking, creative thinking, and problem solving related to particular content areas. Many of the strategies in Chapters 6 and 7 can be used to enhance these reasoning skills as applied to the discipline.

In this model, the main emphasis is on the lesson design, skilled enactment of the lesson, reflective analysis of student learning, and use of analysis to develop future lessons (West, 2009). For example, the gifted education teacher/coach may work with a social studies teacher to emphasize "thinking as a historian" within the lesson design. This might include intentional use of domain-specific academic vocabulary, elements of reasoning (e.g., purpose, points of view, assumptions, and implications of a primary source document), cognitive reasoning that a historian would use, or the application of many of Kaplan's (2009) thinking tools (e.g., multiple perspectives, change over time, trends, rules/structure) to examine a problem in history. The classroom teacher can learn these skills through observing the coach model the strategy, coplanning a lesson, practicing these skills, or reflecting on student learning with support from the coach.

The initial collaboration meeting may include coplanning the lesson or perhaps planning for the gifted education teacher/coach to model the lesson. The teacher and coach would think through these processes together before the classroom teacher implements the lesson, considering how these ways of thinking reveal how historians actually approach their field of study. This is followed by the classroom teacher implementing the lesson and then reflecting on student responses. Because the emphasis is on the discourse of the discipline, the classroom teacher and gifted education teacher/coach may ask, "How do student outcomes reflect the thinking, speaking, and writing of the discipline?" and consider next steps in instruction that would deepen students' skills to not only learn the content, but also learn to process or think about content as a disciplinarian.

Foundational Principles of Coaching

There are key foundational principles that best support successful coaching within a gifted education context. First, a priority is placed on being teacher-centered, not coach-centered. This focus respects teacher autonomy, recognizes teachers' value systems, provides ongoing support, and engages teachers as thinking partners to improve student learning.

Unfortunately, there are those who might resist the coaching process. This is not because they are resistant to change; it is because they feel as though "change" is being forced upon them (Tschannen-Moran & Tschannen-Moran, 2011). Remember, coaching is a form of professional learning for teachers, and as such, classroom teachers should feel as though they are personally involved in the process. This involves including teacher choice and acknowledging teacher value systems (Knight, 2019). By focusing on each of these teacher-focused attributes, trust is better established, leading to greater engagement and buy-in from teachers in the coaching process itself. Therefore, the TEAM frame remains a key component in successful coaching. Aguilar (2013) continued to support this connection by stressing the importance of confidentiality, active listening, vulnerability, and validation in the collaborative coaching process.

Respecting teacher autonomy is also a foundational component to successful coaching. Take a moment to reflect on the demands made on teachers every day. Teachers are provided with exhaustive lists of what to teach, how to teach, and how to discipline their students. Now think about how gifted students react when they are constantly told what to do, how to do it, and how to respond to learning. More often than not, the result is noncompliance, disengagement, and apathy. Likewise, teachers need to make choices as they engage in the coaching process. By providing this autonomy, they are empowered to see how their own choices make a direct impact on their instructional practices within the classroom.

As you engage in coaching conversations, strive to understand the teachers' value systems by what they enjoy most about teaching. What components of their teaching do they see as having the greatest impact? What was the reason behind why they became teachers in the first place? Bambrick-Santoyo (2019) pointed out that teachers practice most what they value, so, in understanding what teachers value most, the coaching process is improved and streamlined.

Coaching is a collaborative process that provides ongoing, consistent, and constructive support. It embraces a shared understanding of setting a goal, planning to meet that goal, and reflecting on how the process went. Through this ongoing process, new goals are refined, identified, and built upon.

Finally, successful coaching recognizes that teachers are thinking partners. Ultimately, the coaching process should not focus on "improving" the classroom teacher. Instead, coaching should focus on improving student learning, where both partners' opinions matter and are valued. One idea to encourage this type of dialogue is to use what Knight (2019) referred to as third points. Third points are samples of student work, video recordings, or similar artifacts that take the focus off the teacher or coach and allow the two professionals to focus on a separate work to guide the coaching conversation. More information on third points is shared later in the chapter.

Developing the Craft of Coaching

Although coaching is highly collaborative, there are nuances that make it distinctively different than collaboration between a classroom teacher and gifted education teacher. For example, when a gifted education teacher and classroom teacher collaborate on creating a lesson to better meet the needs of gifted learners, both teachers are providing insights, contributing ideas, and offering suggestions. As discussed in Chapter 2, this collaboration might also include different roles and responsibilities for each teacher during the instructional design process. As part of the coaching cycle, however, the coach's key responsibility is to lead teachers in the self-discovery process of improving their instructional practice. This means the coach would not outwardly offer insights into lesson design, but instead, would guide teachers to discover and gain new insights about how to improve instructional practice. Without question, the coach is still responsible in helping to set goals, model new strategies, and gauge student progress, but through the coaching process, how the collaborative conversation unfolds is quite different and has unique challenges.

In many ways coaching is like a highly specialized art form. It takes a great deal of training and professional practice to do it well. In the same manner that a professional dancer is able interpret music through movement to help an audience feel an emotion, or a skilled painter is able to capture thoughts, surroundings, and feelings to convey a story in a work of art, a coach is able to help a teacher recognize how to better improve classroom practice through effective questioning, analysis, and reflective thought.

Communication in Coaching

As previously described, there is a nuanced craft to coaching. Coaching begins with listening to what the teacher wants to focus on. Listening can then lead to clarifying, affirming, and activating potential through reflective feedback. These effective components of communication can be used through the coaching conversation (see Resource 11 on p. 137).

Listening With Purpose

Listening with a purpose will pave a path for the coaching process. Everyone needs to feel important, valued, and worthy. This need is amplified when educators make themselves vulnerable in an effort to grow in their instructional practice, which is why it is often difficult for teachers to seek out additional support for meeting the needs of gifted learners. In coaching, a priority should be given to helping collaborative partners feel as though they have your full attention. As such, an underlying purpose in every coaching session should include making the collaborative partner feel appreciated and heard. Continue to value the time set aside for coaching and keep the spotlight on the teacher without being distracted by incoming emails, the next lesson you need to model, or a conversation held earlier in the day. Be present. Ultimately, the reason for listening with a purpose is to understand where the teacher is and where they want to go. In many ways, active listening serves as the road map to guide the coaching process.

Counterproductive Listening. In order to engage in listening with a purpose, the various types of listening that negatively impact coaching need to be acknowledged. Here, we focus on autobiographical, judgmental, inquisitive, and solution-focused listening (see Costa & Gamston 2015; Kee et al., 2010), and apply them specifically to gifted education coaching contexts. In each of these counterproductive types of listening, the coach is not committed to understanding what the speaker is sharing, leading to missed opportunities for reflective practice.

Autobiographical Listening. Because of our need to relate to others, it can be easy to fall into the autobiographical listening trap (see Figure 7). Although this type of listening is not always detrimental, it does not align with the foundations of strong coaching. Initially, through autobiographical listening, a person tunes in to what the speaker is sharing, but then interjects a personal story as a way to connect. This has a detrimental impact because the listener is focusing on their own frame of reference instead of trying to understand what the speaker is trying to share (Covey, 1989/2015). Coaching should focus on building capacity in another teacher's instructional practice, so if the story is turned away from the teacher and onto the coach, the session becomes coach-centered instead of teacher-centered.

Judgmental Listening. Judgmental listening (see Figure 8) involves the coach targeting the perceived flaws or greatness of a person, resulting in inner dialogue that takes over during the listening process. From this inner dialogue, a positive response from the coach can emit an authoritarian tone, whereas a negative response can reduce creativity and inspiration in the classroom teacher. This type of judgmental listening can lead to coming across as arrogant (Kee et al., 2010) or that "my way is the right way." As such, it is detrimental to collaborative practice and has long-lasting, negative effects.

Inquisitive Listening. Through inquisitive listening (see Figure 9), the coach is focused on their own desire to know "why" a situation is occurring instead of purposefully listening to what the teacher is sharing. The resulting "why" spiral can deter from the focus of coaching. This leads to conversations that do not align with the original goal and purpose which were established through the Collaborative

FIGURE 7
Autobiographical Listening

Classroom Teacher	Counterproductive Response
"In my gifted cluster class, I have a few students who race through their work and start causing distractions to the other students in the classroom."	"Oh, I can totally relate! I remember when I was teaching fourth grade and had to reexamine how I differentiated my classroom assignments to deal with the same problem."

Implications
By interjecting a related experience, the classroom teacher's opportunity for self-reflection and discovery are sabotaged. In addition, this counterproductive response does not presume positive intent and creates a sense of being "better" than the classroom teacher.

FIGURE 8
Judgmental Listening

Classroom Teacher	Counterproductive Response
"When my gifted students finish their work early, I let them become teacher helpers to help the other students in my class who are still struggling."	The coach is thinking to self, "How can this teacher still think it is okay for gifted students to not be challenged, rush through their work, and then spend their classroom time teaching their peers? Doesn't this teacher realize that these gifted students have the right to learn something new, too? This is so frustrating. . . ."

Implications
By engaging in judgmental listening, the inner dialogue of the coach is preventing listening with a purpose. Because of this, the coaching process is impacted by feelings of frustration. This inner dialogue is detrimental to presuming positive intent, impedes the coach's ability to guide self-discovery, and results in condescending coaching conversations.

> **FIGURE 9**
> Inquisitive Listening
>
> | Classroom Teacher | Counterproductive Response |
> | --- | --- |
> | "After seeing you model how to use concept mapping as a preassessment tool, I tried it, but it didn't give me the results I was hoping for to help me in my classroom differentiation." | Questions might evolve in this manner: "In what areas do you feel like the preassessment did not provide you with the information you needed? Which students stood out amongst your class? In what ways do your gifted students usually stand out in your class? What behaviors impede their learning? Given that the same students act out in class, how might you adjust your classroom seating?" |
>
> | Implications |
> | --- |
> | In this scenario, there are some positive takeaways. The coaching questions presumed positive intent, and it seems as though a positive collaborative relationship has been established. The coach seemed genuinely interested in helping the classroom teacher, but the problem stemmed from how the questions departed from the original concern about preassessments and ended on classroom seating. |

Process Model. Stay focused on the quality and purpose of questions throughout the coaching process.

Solution-Focused Listening. At the heart of every coach is the desire to help fellow teachers. In solution-focused listening (see Figure 10), the coach is intently focused on how to solve the problem instead of listening to what the teacher is sharing. Take a moment to reflect on past grade-level meetings you have had as a classroom teacher. Quite often during these meetings, when a teacher shares about a struggle within the classroom, a fellow colleague steps forward with advice and instructional strategies to address that problem. The intention might be good, but this can undermine the ability of the classroom teacher to reflect and grow within their own instructional practice.

Coaching Through Committed Listening. By listening for understanding, committed listening leads to productive collaboration (Gross Cheliotes & Reilly, 2010; Kee et. al., 2010). Committed listening means keeping the conversation focused on what the classroom teacher wants to discuss. In the context of gifted education, this might include building capacity for curriculum compacting, analyzing pre- and postassessment data, or serving gifted students from culturally, linguistically, and economically diverse (CLED) backgrounds. To open doors for commit-

---

FIGURE 10
Solution-Focused Listening

Classroom Teacher	Counterproductive Response
"I have one student in my class who already knows our entire next unit in math. I don't know how I am going to keep him engaged."	The coach is thinking to self, "This is a great opportunity for me to set up the I-LEARN process for independent study with this student. First, I will . . ."

Implications	
Although meaning well, solution-focused listening denies the classroom teacher the opportunity to problem solve how to best meet the student's needs. If given the chance, the classroom teacher would have quickly recognized that independent study was a viable option. Then, the coaching session could have focused on how to work through that process, helping the teacher gain valuable knowledge on how to proceed with that option.	

---

ted listening, it may be helpful to ask, "At the end of this conversation, what would you like to happen?" The response might be as simple as, "I just needed to vent and have someone listen to me," but there might be other times that the response includes, "I need some options" or "I need to brainstorm." Regardless, the teacher will feel valued and heard.

Coaching through committed listening also seeks to understand the underlying issue behind whatever emotion is driving the speaker. If the speaker is upset, the best response might be to validate the feelings involved and "witness the struggle" (Kee et al., 2010). If the coach's response consists of, "It's going to be okay," it devalues the feelings involved. Instead, responding with, "This is a difficult situation to navigate right now" validates the teacher's experience. Through committed listening, the focus continues to be on understanding what has brought our collaborative partners to where they currently are in order to guide reflection on their next steps.

Paraphrasing is an effective tool to demonstrate committed listening to both emotions and content being shared. Paraphrasing can focus on acknowledging and clarifying, summarizing, and shifting conceptual focus (Costa & Gamston, 2015; Kee et al., 2010; Lipton & Wellman, 2001). Unlike conventional wisdom, paraphrasing should not start with "What I hear you saying is. . . ." Instead, the focus should be directly on the listener, showing that you are listening and understanding (or trying to understand) what is being shared (Kee et al., 2010). Examples of types of paraphrasing that might apply to coaching in gifted education are indicated in Table 21.

TABLE 21
Types of Paraphrasing Applied to Coaching in Gifted Education Contexts

Type of Paraphrase	Support Given	Example
Clarifying and Acknowledging	Identify the emotion conveyed and content shared: + You're feeling . . . + You're thinking that . . . + You're wondering . . .	+ You're frustrated because the student has such a high IQ but does very little work in class. + You are feeling overwhelmed with the variety of learners' needs in your classroom.
Summarizing and Organizing	When the speaker does a great deal of talking, this can help them understand how their thoughts are organized rather than scrambled together: + On one hand . . . on the other . . . + First you will . . . then . . .	+ On one hand, you would like to try to develop tiered assignments, but you are concerned with how much planning time this will involve. + You are working through two main challenges: You don't want the nonidentified gifted students feeling different than others, and you are wondering how parents will respond to differentiated assignments.
Conceptual Shift	Identify beliefs, values, assumptions, and perspectives to lead the listener to new ideas or clarify their thinking: + You seem to value . . . + A major goal for you is . . . + You are concerned overall . . .	+ So it seems you value equity in your classroom—every child deserves to learn something new every day. + Given your concern that some learners already know the content you will teach, you are thinking you need to develop a preassessment that would help you decide what to do for these learners.

Note. Supports for types of paraphrases are adapted from Kee et al. (2010).

Reflective Feedback: Ask, Affirm, and Activate

Much of this chapter has focused on effective communication skills, most importantly, listening and valuing what is shared. As you show committed listening through coaching conversations, how then do you guide the teacher toward the "aha" moments, insights, and self-discoveries on what to actually do? This comes through the nuanced skill of using information from listening to provide reflective feedback. Perkins (2003) explained that this includes asking clarifying questions, valuing potential, and asking reflective questions. While applying the principle of positive intent in all parts of reflective feedback (see Chapter 2), coaches can lead the classroom teacher to uncover new insights of understanding that ultimately lead to the teacher taking action. We have adapted these types of feedback (Perkins, 2003) to the following:

1. **Ask questions for focus:** These questions help bring focus to the conversation and ensure the coach and listener are both on the same page.
2. **Affirm the positive and potential:** These statements attend to strengths and possibilities of ideas explored.
3. **Activate potential:** These questions lead the conversation toward uncovering alternatives, other points of view, and self-directed options.

Resource 11: Collaborative Process Model for Coaching in Gifted Education provides examples of types of questions and feedback that might be used throughout a coaching conversation.

Actionable Feedback

In some contexts, there is a fine line between coaching and consulting. Perhaps there are times when a balance needs to be provided between reflective feedback and actionable feedback. If the coaching situation is one that involves the classroom teacher learning and applying a new skill through a gradual release of responsibility (as in the models discussed at the beginning of the chapter), the coach may offer questions or feedback that connects teacher behavior to how students responded in a lesson. For example, a coach might ask, "When you _____ , how did students respond?" This helps teachers see the causal link between their actions and student learning. Descriptive feedback can also be provided: "I noticed when you _____ , students _____" (Feldman, 2016). Such feedback should remain descriptive, not evaluative, leading to deeper levels of insight into how instructional practice impacts student learning. Coaches can activate insight for other possibilities by posing, "What do you suppose might happen if . . . ?" (e.g., "What might happen if students were grouped differently?").

Coaching Through Third Points

One unique challenge in coaching to build capacity in gifted instructional practices is that quite often, classroom teachers have had little to no gifted training as part of their preservice education or ongoing professional learning. Without this

Collaborative Process Model for Coaching in Gifted Education

Example Questions and Statements

Consider use of standards, case studies, work samples, videos, demonstration, observation, and other "third point tools" as a point of reference for dialogue.		
	Ask Questions for Focus	**Affirm Potential and Positives**	**Activate Possibilities**
Purpose Start with a teacher-selected purpose. Key Question: What is the desired outcome you would like to have from this coaching session?	+ Which area would you like to continue to explore in your instructional practice? + When you reflect on last quarter, what areas of growth would you like to continue to pursue? + Given the information shared at our last institute day, what piqued your interest?	+ Your goal for students to extend their thinking beyond the standards is a great place to start. + You have really thought through assessment options to understand student learning. + Your desire to understand more about underachievement will pave a path for student success.	+ To align most closely to best practices in gifted education, how might your focus connect to ____ ? + What would happen if you also considered . . . ? + What effects do you expect to see in student learning, based on this goal?
Plan Guide next steps for growth. Key Question: What methods should be considered to meet your goal?	+ What evidence do we need to collect to see if an impact is being made? + In what ways might you want to learn or refine this skill (e.g., seeing it modeled, through practice with feedback)? What resources will you need? + In what ways can we gather data (e.g., video recording, student work, observations) to determine ____ ?	+ Your plan provides a number of ways for students to show what they know. + The scaffolding will provide opportunities for learners to access high level content. + This idea will really expose them to the way a disciplinarian thinks about this issue.	+ What are you considering for management of tiering? + As you think about what we know about gifted learners, what strategies are you considering that will challenge them beyond their comfort zone? + To align more closely to what we know about infusing creativity with content, how might . . . ?

	Ask Questions for Focus	Affirm Potential and Positives	Activate Possibilities
Reflection Offer reflection for self-direction and next steps. Key Question: How did the plan impact student learning, and what are your next steps?	+ In what ways can we continue to explore this area? + Which area of our plan had the greatest impact in improving professional practice? + What was most challenging?	+ It is clear that when you implemented this strategy, students were engaged. + As an advocate for gifted learners, it is exciting to see how they responded to your instruction. They did not know the answers right away.	+ How can I best support you as you consider an intentional focus on differentiation for gifted learners? + What would be most helpful to you in meeting your goals to effectively differentiate for gifted learners? + What next step will allow students to show their learning to an authentic audience?

Note. The example questions and statements are adapted from Perkins (2003) and Kee et al. (2010).

background, classroom teachers have trouble recognizing or connecting to areas that they have no training in as part of the self-discovery process. In fact, novice teachers have reported that teaching gifted students ranks in the top 25% of challenges that they face within their classrooms (Burkman, 2012). This presents a unique challenge for coaching within the gifted education context, as learner characteristics and models of gifted education are quite different than what are found in the regular education classroom. In recognizing this potential barrier, we suggest a variety of "third point" coaching tools for increasing professional learning focused on the needs of gifted learners.

Third point tools allow coaching conversations to focus on informational documents, videos, student work, and artifacts for reflection rather than evaluatively focusing on the teacher. For example, after modeling a lesson for a classroom teacher, Resource 5: Observing Instructional Strategies for Gifted Learners (p. 68) can serve as a third point coaching tool for guiding reflective dialogue on how instruction impacted student learning. In addition, observation tools such as the Coaching Tool for Classrooms Supporting Gifted Education (see Chapter 10, p. 172) can be used to guide reflection on how physical environment, classroom interactions, curriculum, and assessment practices support students from diverse backgrounds. Although there are a multitude of third point coaching tools, these and those that follow are easily adapted to any context.

Standards as Coaching Tools

In raising awareness of best practice in gifted education, you may begin with something as simple as the NAGC's (2019) Gifted Programming Standards. Classroom teachers are no strangers to standards, but they might not be aware of how the Gifted Programming Standards align with the state standards from which they focus their classroom instruction. The following questions provide a starting point to engage in dialogue through presuming positive intent, while also strengthening an understanding of gifted learners:

+ What stands out to you about the Gifted Programming Standards?
+ Which areas do you see as being the most easily integrated within your grade-level standards? Which areas do you see as the most challenging?
+ In what ways might you integrate Standard "X" into your instructional practice?
+ Which content areas do you feel are most easily addressed through the Gifted Programming Standards? Which do you feel are the most difficult?

As well as a third point coaching tool, the Gifted Programming Standards serve as a means for teachers to reflect on professional learning while keeping student outcomes in mind (Lewis et al., 2018).

Case Studies as Coaching Tools

Case studies are another practical option to consider while building capacity in teachers to recognize the needs of gifted learners. Case studies provide an opportunity to focus a conversation on the provided scenario as a means to identify gifted learner characteristics, the need for differentiation, teacher instructional practices, and the implications of different instructional practices. By focusing the conversation in this manner, there is less of a threat to the classroom teacher, as the dialogue is not directed toward teaching in their own classroom. Although there are many books focused on case studies within education, there are several that are specifically geared toward meeting the needs of gifted learners (e.g., Weber et al., 2014) and how to best differentiate instruction for gifted learners (e.g., Weber et al., 2016). Most published case studies are accompanied by discussion and reflection questions, but consider these general questions that might be applied to coaching through the gifted lens:

+ What stood out to you about gifted education as you read this case study?
+ What challenges/successes were evident for the gifted student(s)?
+ What challenges/successes were evident for the classroom teacher?
+ As someone who works with students who are similar to those in this case study, what parallels did you see to your own classroom?
+ Which strategy seemed to engage the gifted student(s) the most in this scenario?

Another benefit to using case studies as third point coaching tools is that the coach and teacher can seek out case studies specific to the current context to discuss. For instance, if a current teacher wants to improve teaching practices for reaching culturally diverse students or twice-exceptional students, specific case studies can be read and discussed that reflect similar classroom attributes. With that being said, note that all gifted learners are uniquely different, so the conversation needs to acknowledge that gifted education is not a one-size-fits-all solution. Also, when using case studies, make sure that the teacher has time to read and process the case study before the coaching session. Teachers should never feel as though they are "on the spot" in having to discuss a scenario that the coach has had time to read and reflect upon, but they are seeing for the first time. This is detrimental in creating the shared dialogue necessary for successful coaching.

Student Work Samples as Coaching Tools

Student work samples are another valuable tool in building an understanding of gifted learners' strengths, talents, and needs. In some ways, student work samples are a bit more limiting than case studies or video recordings, as they often do not include the students' thoughts "behind" the assignment. For this reason, we strongly encourage anyone who will be using student work samples as third points to have students include written reflections on each assignment. These reflections might include what they found most engaging about the assignment, what they valued most about the assignment, what they would do differently if given the opportunity, or what was most challenging about the assignment. These types of reflections are common in selecting work for portfolios and provide an opportunity for students to share their level of engagement and communicate greater knowledge of what the work sample meant to them (Danielson, 2008).

When using student work samples as third points, the focus should be on learning what the gifted students valued from the activity, what kept them engaged, what challenged them, and how the teacher would modify the assignment if given the opportunity. Specific attention should also be given to how the assignment was presented to the class and how feedback was provided throughout the learning experience. Suggested questions for discussing student work samples are shared in Table 22.

In addition to Table 22, the following are more generalized questions in regard to work samples as third point coaching tools:

+ What components allow for students to learn content more deeply?
+ In what ways does this student work sample address NAGC (2019) Gifted Programming Standards (e.g., Learning Environments, Curriculum and Instruction)?
+ Which areas of this assignment allow twice-exceptional learners to access the content (or what parts need to be modified)?
+ If the gifted student felt limited on this assignment, in what ways might this activity be adjusted to provide more challenge, harness their interests, or capitalize on their strengths?
+ How are the student's interests, strengths, and learning needs revealed in their reflections?

Regardless of the coaching tool, the collaborative dialogue should be focused on how to build capacity to better recognize the strengths and needs of gifted learners in order to address them.

TABLE 22
Guiding Questions for Gifted Work Samples

Type of Student Work Sample	Potential Guiding Questions for Coaching Collaboration
Characterization Essay With Accompanying Rubric	+ In what ways does the accompanying rubric limit and/or challenge gifted learners? + What do you notice about how the gifted student organized their thoughts? + What might the student need in order to continue to refine their writing skills towards more sophistication?
STEM Project	+ Given the parameters that were provided on this project, what components do you think challenged students to practice thinking, speaking, and writing as those in STEM fields? + In what ways did this project encourage open inquiry and perspective-taking? + In what ways does this prepare the gifted student for next steps in more advanced math and science courses?
Independent Study Project	+ What aspects of this independent study incorporate depth and complexity of learning? + In understanding that this work sample is from a fifth grader, what components of the activity signify this student is working above grade-level expectations? + How does this assignment encourage the development of psychosocial skills (e.g., perseverance, goal attainment, organization)? How does it encourage self-reflection of learning?

Coaching Through the Collaborative Process Model: Putting It All Together

Set a purpose. Plan. Reflect. The Collaborative Process Model, along with committed listening and the foundational components of being learner focused, promoting self-discovery, and providing ongoing support, all contribute to successful coaching practice. Here, we offer a structure for putting together the essential components of effective coaching as they fit in the context of the Collaborative Process Model. Through each step, the coach's role is to listen, clarify, affirm, and guide the classroom teacher to come to realizations of their potential. This model may be applied in a variety of ways, depending on the coaching model used. In instructional coaching, this process involves a plan for learning or refining new skills.

+ **Set a purpose:** Coaching sessions should begin with a teacher-selected purpose. This might be to manage classroom behaviors, develop preassessments, compact curriculum, or other various tasks. If the teacher has difficulty narrowing down the purpose, the coach may refer to the "asking for focus" questions provided on Resource 11.

+ **Plan:** Once the purpose of the coaching session is set, it is much easier to guide the teacher into recognizing next steps for continued growth. This also includes exploring methods the teacher might consider for achieving their goal, such as:
  o reading related research,
  o observing the coach model a skill or strategy,
  o practicing a skill in the classroom with guided feedback from the coach,
  o collecting and reflecting on student data to determine next steps,
  o conversing about a particular problem or issue, and
  o examining a third point coaching tool (e.g., the NAGC [2019] Gifted Programming Standards, case studies, videos, student work, etc.).

  Be prepared for this phase to span over a period of time, as it is quite different than the "plan" process of creating a lesson for a coteaching lesson. Remember, this is professional learning to build capacity, and that does not happen in one coaching session.

+ **Reflection:** This component of the Collaborative Process Model is perpetual throughout the coaching process. Whether a lesson has been modeled, data have been collected, or student work is being assessed, reflection should guide the next steps.

Although we provide a structure to follow on Resource 11, the process is meant to be fluid. At each step (purpose, plan, reflection), effective coaching starts with sufficient time for listening and creates space for the participating teacher to unravel thoughts around a goal or issue. Then, the coach focuses the conversation on the self-directed issue while affirming the values and positive possibilities of what is being shared. This may bring the coach back to asking focus questions before posing questions that evoke "aha" moments and realizations that eventually provide momentum for future action. A coach's flexibility and nuanced skill in asking thought-provoking questions are keys to unlocking classroom teachers' potential.

Chapter 9

Collaborative Consultation

Developing Specialized Supports for Gifted Students

    This chapter provides a process for applying collaborative consultation while working with teachers, parents, counselors, school psychologists, and other school personnel who might be involved in addressing special needs of gifted students. When issues such as learning disabilities, underachievement, perfectionism, or anxiety inhibit student learning, you may work with a team in collaborative problem solving to consider an appropriate individualized plan for the student. Although there are entire books dedicated to these issues, this chapter highlights important questions and strategies to consider when working with others to develop specialized supports or interventions in response to students' needs. Many of these strategies are foundational to collaboration efforts aimed at serving students either directly or indirectly.

    So far, we have explained the collaborative roles of coteaching and coaching in gifted education. In this chapter, we emphasize collaborative consultation in which the gifted education teacher, gifted coordinator, or district gifted consultant provides advice or guidance to others based on their expertise in working with gifted students. For consultation to be truly collaborative, decisions should be made with others to identify the student's need, determine an appropriate plan of action, and evaluate effectiveness. This endeavor is not collaborative if the consultant solely makes such decisions.

You may find that a large part of the consultative role is to advocate for students by addressing myths and misconceptions often associated with what giftedness "looks like." For example, giftedness can be masked by a disability in twice-exceptional students. Further, when gifted underachievers underperform, you may face questions about whether the gifted student even "deserves" unique adjustments to curriculum. In addressing such misconceptions, you can emphasize enhancing student strengths over remediating deficits and explain how motivation intersects with high intellectual ability during collaborative consultation.

The steps of the Collaboration Process Model can serve as a structure for facilitating plans of action to address special concerns. Setting the purpose involves understanding the need or problem to be addressed. The planning step revolves around considering the student's strengths, matching interventions to the student's need, and detailing who will do what and how progress will be measured. The reflection step includes evaluating the effectiveness of the plan, considering revisions, and determining next steps. These steps with specific questions to consider are outlined in Table 23.

The TEAM frame continues to apply to collaborative consultation as well. All members should have a shared understanding of their roles, timelines, and expectations for supporting the student. Trust is established through a collective commitment to accountability and follow-through of the collaborative plan. Collaborators can intentionally engage to leverage the strengths and expertise of each team member and align values to focus on removing barriers to develop a student's gifts and talents. The team can maintain the effectiveness of the collaborative work through ongoing reports of progress and open dialogue about what's working and what's not.

This structure provides the foundation for facilitating conversations concerning gifted students who need additional support to be successful and achieve. In the sections that follow, we highlight many special concerns that interfere with a student's achievement. The supports and strategies mentioned in these sections are not exhaustive, yet we aim to provide a starting place that can lead to further exploration in additional resources.

Twice-Exceptional Learners

Twice-exceptional (2e) learners are those who have two or more exceptionalities that impact their learning. With one exceptionality being recognized as giftedness, coexisting disabilities might be one or more of the 14 disabilities recognized by the Individuals With Disabilities Education Act (IDEA, 1990), excluding any cognitive disability. These might include learning disabilities, Attention-Deficit/Hyperactivity

TABLE 23

Collaborative Process Model Steps for Collaborative Consultation

Collaborative Steps	Questions to Consider
Set a Purpose: Establish purpose of collaboration: Develop supports and interventions for an identified need. Aim to understand the need.	+ What concerns do we have for the student? + What is the desired outcome for this student? + What data do we need in order to understand the issue or need? + What are the causes of ____ ? In what contexts do we see ____ ? + What are the effects of ____ ? + What do we need to address first?
Plan Intervention: Explore, choose, and implement strategies.	+ What are the student's strengths? How might this inform our plan? + What strategies might we consider? + How will this be done? Who will do what? + How will we monitor progress for the student?
Reflect: Follow up and evaluate the plan and student progress. Make revisions to interventions as needed.	+ What changes were made? + How is the student responding to the supports/ interventions? + What adjustments do we need to make? + How can we ensure continued success?

Disorder (ADHD), behavioral disabilities, emotional disabilities, autism spectrum disorders, or various other health impairments.

While working collaboratively to best address the learning needs of twice-exceptional learners, remember the popular saying, "If you have met one twice-exceptional student, you have met one twice-exceptional student." This, in part, is due to the fact that not only does their giftedness coexist with various other disabilities, but also it is often coupled with the anxiety and/or underachievement factors discussed later in this chapter. Due to the complexity of these needs, the collaborative team should include members beyond classroom teachers, such as school psychologists, social workers, school counselors, and various special education teachers.

Identification

Through consultation, continue to work with your team to develop an understanding of what it means to be twice-exceptional, and raise awareness for the following factors that impede gifted identification for this population:

+ A student's giftedness can "mask" other exceptionalities. In these cases, a student is able to meet grade-level expectations, but the student's cognitive ability far exceeds grade-level standards. For example, a student with a reading disability might be able to read at grade level because giftedness compensates for the learning disability, but the student might perform at a higher level if both areas of exceptionality were diagnosed and supported.

+ A student's disability can "mask" giftedness. In these cases, a student might have sensory or communication disabilities that impede the student from demonstrating intellectual giftedness (Robinson et al., 2007). In this case, a student's language delay could impact articulating advanced levels of learning.

+ A student might have multiple combinations of exceptionalities in addition to giftedness. This might present as a student who is diagnosed with ADHD, experiences generalized anxiety disorder, and has a learning disability. With so many factors affecting a student's learning, it is often difficult to ascertain giftedness.

+ Response to Intervention (RtI), a diagnostic approach for identifying students with exceptionalities, no longer considers significant discrepancies between a student's potential and performance as a way of identifying learning disabilities. This further complicates the identification process (Assouline et al., 2010; Assouline & Whiteman, 2011) because although the twice-exceptional student appears to be achieving, they are actually working well below their potential. In addition, RtI makes the assumptions that "broadly appropriate" curriculum is best practice for gifted learners and that baselines for gifted learners are the same as those for average or below-average learners (NAGC, n.d.). As a result, meaningful data collection for twice-exceptional diagnosis becomes increasingly more difficult.

With the increased awareness of these factors, the team's next steps should be on the shared responsibility of contributing specialized insights to the identification process. While evaluating various methods of data collection for twice-exceptional diagnosis (e.g., standardized tests, surveys, classroom assessments, interviews, classroom observations), team members should remain mindful that gifted learners are often gifted in just one content area (e.g., math, writing, creativity, etc.) as they examine students' academic profiles and social-emotional characteristics (NAGC, n.d.). Table 24 outlines potential questions to help guide these collaborative discussions.

In addition to the insights gained from these discussions, review students' school records with your team, looking for any patterns of academic strengths and weaknesses that warrant further attention (Assouline et al., 2006). Ultimately, a comprehensive evaluation not only lays the foundation for identifying twice-exceptional

TABLE 24
Questions to Develop Comprehensive Evaluations for Twice-Exceptional Identification

Educational Specialist	Potential Questions to Guide Shared Decision Making
Classroom Teacher	+ Which content standards is the student having the most difficulty mastering? What content standards is the student most successful at mastering?
	+ When the process for demonstrating mastery of a concept is changed, does the student's level of understanding seem to change? For example, does the student have difficulty demonstrating mastery on an essay test, but excel when given the opportunity to share through an oral presentation?
	+ When given choice, does the student consistently gravitate to particular options?
School Counselor/ Social Worker	+ In knowing that many twice-exceptional students experience performance anxiety, what strategies can be implemented to help the student do their best during test administration for formal identification?
	+ How might we best communicate an understanding of what it means to be a twice-exceptional learner to the student, keeping in mind that many of these students refuse accommodations because they often feel they are intellectually cheating (Baum et al., 2006)?
School Psychologist/ Diagnostician	+ Which cognitive assessment provides the best opportunity for a student who has difficulty with language to demonstrate their high cognitive ability? Is there a particular nonverbal assessment that might work best?
	+ Are there large discrepancies between subtest scores on the *same* assessment? How might these discrepancies inform gifted identification for twice-exceptional learners?
	+ On cognitive assessments, in what ways do subtests impact full-scale scores? For example, if a student has low scores in working memory and processing speed, how will this impact overall scores for gifted identification or qualification for gifted services? How can we best address this impact?
	+ In understanding that discrepancies between potential and performance are indicative of twice-exceptionality (Assouline & Whiteman, 2011), in what areas, if any, does this student show discrepancy between achievement and ability scores?
Special Education Teacher	+ Which accommodations might be most successful for this particular student? For example, if a student is diagnosed with dyslexia, an appropriate accommodation might be to have text read aloud during assessments. (It is very important that this discussion is directly related to each individual student, as each student presents with unique needs for accommodations. This should *never* be a discussion based on stereotypes of different disabilities.)
	+ How has the student responded to special education services?
	+ What do you notice about the student's strengths, weaknesses, and interests?

learners, but also creates a path for creating positive learning environments for twice-exceptional students to work through their areas of strength and receive appropriate accommodations for their disabilities (Foley-Nicpon et al., 2011; Reis et al., 2014).

Meeting the Needs

Once twice-exceptional students have been identified, collaborative efforts should focus on meeting their needs within the classroom. When determining an appropriate plan of action through collaborative consultation, continue to stress the importance of a strength-based approach. Educators may initially focus on the disability alone. Although this stems from good intentions as an attempt to "fix" the deficit, it has long-lasting effects on the individual, as typical interventions consisting of review activities, simplified activities, and remedial lessons are counterproductive for twice-exceptional learners (Reis et al., 2014).

Strength-Based Interventions. Perspective-taking is important in understanding the needs of twice-exceptional learners. If you think of something that's difficult for you to do or perform, how might you feel if the work you did every day had to be demonstrated through that area of weakness, without ever being able to share a talent or work through an area of interest? Over time, this would potentially impact how you value your ability to accomplish goals, resulting in negative repercussions. Twice-exceptional students feel the same way when they are constantly asked to work through their area of weakness. To address this issue through strength-based interventions, the team should identify a student's strengths and recognize when the student is most successful in learning. These strengths can then be used to address a student's area(s) of weakness. For example, if a student is highly theatrical and consistently engaged in role-playing scenarios, but has difficulty with reading comprehension, the team might decide to incorporate more reader's theater, appropriately leveled plays, or simulations for the student to continue to build those comprehension skills.

When discussing strength-based interventions, a common question that often surfaces is, "When and how will the student ever learn the foundational skills needed to work through the area(s) of weakness?" The answer to this question stems from understanding how twice-exceptional students learn. Twice-exceptional learners do not respond to remediation in the same manner as typical students receiving special education services. Through collaborative consultation, continue to help the team recognize that twice-exceptional learners master the more complex, conceptual information more easily than drilled, skill-focused learning (Hughes, 2011), and as such, conceptual understanding should be the first step in remediation efforts. This is in contrast to remediation for other students receiving special education services, which is typically focused on continued repetition and practice on foundational skills.

TABLE 25

Suggestions for Twice-Exceptional Supported Learning

Concept Focus	Advanced Process	Advanced Content
+ Prioritize conceptual understanding over remediation. + Use the concept attainment strategy and concept development model to develop deep understandings (see Chapter 7). + Connect universal generalizations to any remediated content. + For students who need support for reading comprehension, incorporate photos, artwork, and other visuals to develop conceptual understanding. + Incorporate frequent feedback and check-ins to monitor students' conceptual understanding.	+ In using graphic organizers as scaffolds for learning, integrate elements of reasoning, Kaplan's (2009) thinking tools, or other models to organize thinking (see Chapter 6). + Create checklists for applying models of thinking to content (e.g., checklist for SCAMPER, dimension of creative thinking; see Chapter 6). + Integrate metaphorical stretch thinking into prompts/assignments for students with dyslexia, as these learners tend to have strengths in abstract thinking (see Chapter 6). + When working with manipulatives, connect the learning process with how disciplinarians in the field approach new learning (e.g., experts often build and test models and prototypes). + Use frames as scaffolds for students to articulate and support their reasoning (see Chapter 10).	+ Select texts that focus on depth vs. length (e.g., analyze a thought-provoking shorter poem vs. a longer poem). + Add depth and complexity to modified content through Kaplan's (2009) thinking tools (see Chapter 6). + Integrate critical thinking into modified research by integrating visual images as part of the research process (e.g., work from clues in an antique photo). + Use sites such as Newsela to adjust Lexile levels on the same advanced content-focus as other gifted peers.

Note. Adapted from *Addressing the Needs of Twice-Exceptional Learners Template*, by V. Phelps, 2020, Sumner County Schools. Adapted with permission of the author.

This reverse hierarchy approach should be used when planning to meet the needs of twice-exceptional learners. In essence, the reverse hierarchy places priority on conceptual understandings first and then on compensation strategies through advanced processes and advanced content. Table 25 provides suggestions of how to

TABLE 26

Reframing Negative Behavior Connotations Into Positive Instructional Strategies

Negative Behavior Connotations →	Positive Behavior Connotations →	Instructional Strategies
Impulsive, lack of restraint	Risk-taker, adventurous	+ Simulations + Dimensions of Creative Thinking
Talks excessively	Strong skills in debate and oral presentations	+ Debate + Role-playing + Reader's Theater
Difficulty with changes in routine	Highly skilled at following literal directions	+ Concept Attainment Strategy + Double Fishbone
Fidgety, frequent movement	Excels in hands-on tasks	+ 3-D Model Representations + Engineering Tasks
Difficulty working with others	Strong, autonomous learner	+ Self-Selected Graduated Difficulty + Independent Study through the I-LEARN Process

support twice-exceptional students' learning in this manner. Through the process of collaborative consultation, continue to seek active involvement from the special education teachers on the team to explore which types of support strategies (e.g., graphic organizers, explicit instruction, assistive technology, checklists, fill-in notes, visuals, etc.) to use alongside gifted programming, as the team seeks to empower twice-exceptional learners.

Reframing Negative Connotations. Unfortunately, negative connotations associated with disabilities often become the focus as teams navigate interventions. Instead, focus on how the behaviors can be used to identify a student's strengths (Baum & Schader, 2018). Table 26 provides an example of how these negative connotations can be reframed into positive connotations, leading to effective learning experiences for twice-exceptional learners.

Finally, as part of collaborative consultation, schedule ongoing, reflective, follow-up sessions with the team to evaluate student progress and make any revisions to the student's learning plan. During these collaborative conversations, identify how the student has been responding to instructional supports and make any needed adjustments. Continue to stress the importance of working through a student's strengths to address any areas of weakness.

Underachievement

Underachievement occurs when there is a significant discrepancy between actual achievement and expected achievement. Underachievement is a complex problem and can be misunderstood among classroom teachers and others working with the student. As previously mentioned, some may assume that gifted underachievers do not "deserve" gifted services or individualized curriculum options if they are underperforming. Through collaboration, you can help build awareness to why gifted students underachieve and develop a plan to address it.

Underachievement is like a skin rash—as educators we see the symptoms, but the root cause is much more difficult to uncover (Delisle, 2018). Just as a rash can be caused by an allergic reaction to food, a virus, or heat, underachievement is caused by a number of underlying factors. The Achievement Orientation Model (Siegle & McCoach, 2005) provides guidance for understanding and reversing underachievement. In this model, developed with gifted underachievers in mind, the motivation to achieve is influenced by environmental perception ("Can I be successful here? Am I supported?"), self-efficacy ("Do I believe I can do this?"), and goal valuation ("Is this task worthwhile and meaningful?"). The interaction of these factors ignites the motivation and self-regulation skills to work hard and achieve (Siegle et al., 2017). In other words, the ability to control one's thoughts, emotions, and behaviors to pursue long-term goals is the resulting factor of feeling supported, having confidence in one's abilities, and valuing the task at hand.

Before planning ways to address the underachievement, the team should strive to understand and identify which factors are interfering with achievement. While setting a purpose, the team can explore why the student is underachieving. Part of this involves identifying what the student values, known as goal valuation. In Chapter 3, we highlighted the importance of understanding a student's attainment value, intrinsic value, utility value, and cost. When teachers understand the value systems of students, they can consider incorporating these values into a lesson in ways that increase their buy-in. For example, in understanding that a student hopes to pursue a career in the medical field (utility value), the teacher can plan opportunities for the student to engage in content related to the biomedical sciences, encourage involvement in science extracurricular activities, prepare the student for advanced placement science courses, and seek out opportunities for professional mentorships. To understand these values, a simple interest inventory can be used to gain insight into how to better engage students. The National Research Center on the Gifted and Talented (McCoach, n.d.) provided suggestions for questions based on the different types of valuation (attainment, intrinsic, utility, cost):

+ I am most interested in learning about _____ .
+ Doing well in school will help me to _____ .

+ When I am an adult, I want to work as a _____ .
+ When I put forth effort in this class, it's because _____ .
+ I would spend more time on my assignments if _____ .
+ Doing well in this class will help _____ .
+ I feel best/worst about myself when _____ .
+ I am most proud in my learning when _____ .
+ I wish I could _____ .
+ I value _____ .

After collecting student responses from this type of interest inventory (see https://nrcgt.uconn.edu/underachievement_study/goal-valuation/gv_section0 for a more thorough list of questions), the collaborative team is better equipped to identify if students' responses are more geared to their sense of identity, interests, or future goals.

Table 27 provides questions for understanding the issue of underachievement along with strategies that relate directly to the specific components of the Achievement Orientation Model (goal valuation, self-efficacy, environmental perception, and self-regulation). Through exploring the questions and intervention ideas as a collaborative team, an appropriate plan for intervention can be discussed based on the reason for underachievement.

We should also note that sometimes underachievement is seen when the students' needs are twice-exceptional. If that is the case, work with the collaborative team to address the specific academic needs beyond those associated with achievement motivation factors presented here. In the definition of underachievement that follows, underachievement is not the result of a learning disability:

> Underachievers are students who exhibit a severe discrepancy between expected achievement and actual achievement. To be classified as an underachiever, the discrepancy between expected and actual achievement must not be the result of a diagnosed learning disability and must persist over an extended period of time. (Reis & McCoach, 2000, p. 157)

As these interventions are considered and implemented, include the student in this process. As part of the Collaborative Process Model of planning and reflecting on what worked and what did not work well, the student's voice is perhaps the most telling on what next steps should be. As discussed before, understanding the student's value system and tying it to academic objectives can help curb underachievement, but these values are uncovered only if the team listens to the voice of the student. Teams should also consider important questions, such as "What attention does the student get as a result of the underachievement? What are the consequences to

TABLE 27
Questions and Intervention Suggestions for Each Dimension of the Achievement Orientation Model

Dimension	Collaborative Conversation Questions	Intervention Approaches
Goal Valuation	+ What motivates the child outside of school? What does the child value? What are the students' interests and preferences (in and outside of school)? + In what ways has the student had an opportunity to offer their voice into the curriculum, tasks, and assignments?	+ Ask students directly about their motivation. For example, "What would it take for you to engage and be successful in this class?" (Siegle, 2013). Students can be invited into the "change" process by offering feedback on what's working and what's not working well in the environment (Delisle, 2018). + Provide choices in assignments, tasks, and topics. In some cases, it may be necessary to create an individualized learning plan that is codeveloped with the student (Rubenstein et al., 2012). For underachieving students who do not value the task at hand, you must work to understand what they *do* value and embed that within the curriculum. + Explain the purpose for learning any new learning objective and how the learning relates to their present lives and future.
Self-Efficacy	+ What does the student believe about their abilities (and about giftedness)? Does the student adopt more of a fixed mindset or a growth mindset? Does the student believe that their abilities grow from effort or that effort is a sign of inability? + To what extent does the student believe they are capable of achieving success in this area?	+ Promote the idea that *effort* leads to success. Too often, gifted students are successful without working hard in school. They learn that low amounts of effort lead to success, becoming accustomed to feeling valued and successful when things are easy. As curriculum becomes more challenging later, when students must put forth effort, this can lead them to question their abilities. For example, they might think to themselves, "Maybe I'm not really as smart as people think I am if I have to actually work hard on this." Therefore, you must provide challenging learning experiences early on in a student's education that require actual effort. When students understand they have control over their success based on their effort, this promotes a sense of "I can do this," or self-efficacy. + Provide appropriate praise for the process involved in an accomplishment rather than the performance outcome. Help students understand that making a mistake does not equal a lack of potential. Along these same lines, explain the concept of giftedness as a malleable quality that is developed over time (Mofield & Parker Peters, 2018a). Beyond believing that intelligence can grow, when students believe that their academic talents grow when they are stretched beyond their comfort zone, this can mitigate how students deal with setbacks and cultivate a motivation to persevere.

TABLE 27, continued

Dimension	Collaborative Conversation Questions	Intervention Approaches
Environmental Perception	+ Does the student feel the teacher(s) like them? + Does the student feel welcome in class? Why, or why not? + To what extent is the student supported at home? + Talk about the student's perceptions of their classroom environment. Do you think the student feels judged and criticized? Why, or why not?	+ Directly ask students about how they perceive their teachers and their schools' support? Do they feel welcome? + Genuinely show students you value their strengths. Ask, "What do you think you do really well? Do you have an idea for showing me what you know?" + Provide appropriate academic challenge in students' areas of strength. + Allow underachievers to accomplish a learning objective in a different way (proposed by them). This can be a way to increase buy-in and allow them to feel supported.

Self-Regulation	+ To what extent does the student have the organizational skills to be successful?
	+ How does the child self-monitor their own behavior?
	+ Discuss the student's ability to focus. Does the child get distracted easily? Does the student have the "know-how" to stay on-task and achieve set goals?
		+ Teach appropriate organizational skills. Guide students to break tasks down into small steps.
		+ Teach them to problem solve through various alternatives and possible consequences when they encounter obstacles in their work (Mofield & Parker Peters, 2018b).
		+ Guide students to develop clear action plans with small manageable steps toward progress, building in self-rewards for progress along the way.
		+ Help students think about the obstacles in their environment (what they can control and what they cannot control) and develop plans for those obstacles. One strategy to enhance persistence toward reaching a long-term goal is mental contrasting with intentional implementations (Oettingen & Gollwitzer, 2010). The acronym for this is "WOOP."
		  o **Wish:** What is the overall goal to achieve?
		  o **Outcome:** What positive outcomes will come from achieving this goal?
		  o **Obstacle:** What are the possible distractions and circumstances that get in the way of achieving the goal? At this part of WOOP, it is important to discriminate between what is within an individual's control and what is out of their control.
		  o **Plan:** Create an if/then plan for the obstacle. This strategy increases long-term persistence toward a set goal because a plan for tackling obstacles is already in place.

Note. Adapted from *Supporting Gifted Learners' Potential by Addressing Underachievement* [Conference session], by E. Mofield and M. Parker Peters, 2019, Partners in Education Conference, Nashville, TN, United States. Adapted with permission of the authors.

the student's underachievement?" Keep in mind that underachievers may need to play by different "rules" of school. Sometimes, simply doing something "special" outside the norm with this student can itself be an effective approach to curbing underachievement.

Remember that underachievers rarely get empathy from teachers. Gifted underachievers are often looked upon as lazy or undeserving of gifted services. As Delisle (2018) explained, educators must approach these students with dignity. School has often become a place where students simply jump through the hoops and no longer want to play the game of school anymore because they do not see its immediate value in their lives. When collaborating with other teachers and team members, you have an opportunity to advocate for underachievers by explaining they have unique needs that warrant special support.

Perfectionism and Anxiety

You may find yourself conversing with classroom teachers, parents, and school counselors about how a gifted child may be paralyzed by anxiety, overly concerned with making mistakes, or avoiding tasks altogether because of a fear of failure. Perfectionism is often seen in gifted students when self-worth is tied to their achievement. Also, because many gifted students have been praised over and over again for their accomplishments, they may internalize perfection to be a part of their identity. Perfectionism is also akin to anxiety. Given that gifted students have heightened intellectual abilities with high critical thinking skills and abilities to think about long-term implications in the future, gifted students can easily get carried away with "What if?" thinking and all-consuming worry.

Perfectionistic behaviors are classified into two categories: active behaviors and avoidance behaviors (Antony & Swinson, 2009). Active behaviors include striving for a high standard in order to gain a sense of control. This is seen through overtrying and overthinking (e.g., spending 2 hours on an assignment that should have taken 30 minutes), checking and rechecking work, and seeking affirmation and confirmation for work to be correct. Perfectionism is also manifested in avoiding situations that could potentially jeopardize the perfectionist's pursuit of high standards. The avoidance behaviors include procrastination, self-handicapping (e.g., purposefully not doing well on a task while rationalizing, "I could have done it perfectly if I had put more effort into it"), being indecisive, and giving up quickly on a task if it is too difficult.

Related to perfectionism, anxiety is persistent fear or worry that can interfere with an individual's daily functioning. This overwhelming sense of uneasiness is influenced by a number of factors, including feeling pressure to succeed, the child's temperament, stressful life situations, and their environment (including use of social media). Students experiencing anxiety may show restlessness, a drop in grades, loss of sleep, fatigue, avoidance of social situations, irritability, and physical symptoms, such as stomachaches and headaches (National Institute of Mental Health, 2018).

As you continue to work with the collaborative team to help a student manage perfectionism and anxiety, the following questions might be considered (as part of setting a purpose). This sets the stage for understanding when and how perfectionism and/or anxiety occurs:

+ What are ways the student shows perfectionistic behaviors (or anxiety)? Are they active or avoidant behaviors?
+ What contexts seem to make the issue worse?
+ What seems to help the child cope with these issues?
+ In what ways is perfectionism serving as a coping response for other issues (e.g., provides a sense of control, serves as a way to avoid shame)?
+ What do we know about the student's underlying belief system (e.g., "If I am perfect, people will approve of me.")?

In order to know the answer to many of these questions, include the student in the process. After exploring these questions, you can work with the collaborative team to develop a plan by intentionally considering ideas to help the student manage maladaptive perfectionism or anxiety. A few tips are listed in Figure 11 (adapted from Mofield & Parker Peters, 2018b) and Figure 12 (adapted from Mofield & Parker Peters, 2018a) and can be offered in collaboration with school counselors, parents, and classroom teachers on addressing the issue.

Through open dialogue, guided questions, and exploration of strategies, the team can provide support for reframing maladaptive thoughts and beliefs to more functional approaches to dealing with challenges, fears, worry, and perceived failure. Upon reflection, the team may consider if the student may need more intense interventions through professional ongoing therapy or counseling. If the student is diagnosed with generalized anxiety or a related emotional or behavioral disorder, the collaborative team should consider if and how the "disability" creates an adverse impact on the student's learning, considering aforementioned factors mentioned in this chapter around twice-exceptional learners.

Uncovering the Gifts

Through collaborative consultation, you have the opportunity to ask important questions, gather and share information that addresses students' needs, and work with others to continually evaluate how the student is responding to various strate-

FIGURE 11

Tips for Managing Perfectionism

+ Help the student step back and look at the bigger picture. For example, ask, "Looking at all grades together, will one B keep you from being considered a good student? What would happen if this does not go perfectly? Then what? Then what?" until the student reaches the root cause or fear driving the thoughts, emotions, and behaviors (Webb et al., 2005). This can help the child see that in the scheme of the big picture; this is not the "end of the world!"

+ Help the student to think from another person's perspective. For example, you may ask, "Would your friend really think you are less smart if you made a mistake? What would your friend say to you if you made a mistake? Even if you were judged, what would eventually happen?" Thinking through the perspective of how others view mistakes can help the perfectionist realize that they may be magnifying the negative in their thinking.

+ Teach students to recognize negative self-talk and change it to more positive self-talk. For example, "I should have" statements of regret like "I should have done better in my speech" can be changed to "I learned from this experience. Next time I will know to. . . . I don't have control over the past, but I do have control over my next steps."

+ Explicitly teach that there is a difference between healthy and unhealthy types of perfectionism. Healthy perfectionists aim for perfection out of a drive for excellence. Unhealthy perfectionists are consumed with avoiding failure because they feel their self-worth is tied to achieving perfection. Students can be guided to reflect on the motivations behind their behaviors.

+ State to the student, "You do not have to be perfect." Sometimes this simple message needs to be explicitly expressed.

+ Encourage risk-taking. Teachers might assign an achievable risk to a student where there are no high stakes for "failure." For example, this might be encouraging a student to sit with someone new or take a risk in taking an outside-the-box approach to an in-class presentation. When students make the choice to embrace a new challenge, praise these attempts so that risk-taking is reinforced.

+ Develop learning environments where mistakes are valued as part of the learning process. As teachers make mistakes in the classroom, it is important to verbalize mistakes (*Ooops, I forgot to post the prompt to the discussion board*), laugh about them, and "think aloud" through handling the mistake in an adaptive way (*I have to set my timer to remind me to do this every Monday*).

+ Praise effort and the process of learning over the product. Celebrate success by acknowledging growth and learning. Giving *excessive* praise for accomplishments can promote a fixed mindset and risk-avoidance in the future, but it is still important to celebrate the *means* toward accomplishment. In doing so, the focus should be on the incremental achievements along the way and celebration of learning involved.

Note. Adapted from "Shifting the Perfectionist's Mindset: Moving Toward Mindful Excellence," by E. L. Mofield and M. Parker Peters, 2018, *Gifted Child Today, 41*(4), 177–185 (https://doi.org/10.1177/1076217518786989).

FIGURE 12
Tips for Dealing with Anxiety

+ Because gifted learners think in "big ideas," this can be overwhelming in the context of handling emotions. Breaking down the situation to help them process the situation in smaller pieces can help them manage their emotions (e.g., "What exactly happened? What are your concerns about this? What emotions are you feeling about this in particular?").

+ Help a student create a plan for immediate next steps. People often have anxiety over things in their lives that they cannot control. When a plan is made, it gives individuals a sense of control over themselves and their environment.

+ Help the student identify and understand the physical responses that accompany the feeling of anxiety. Perhaps the student has sweaty palms or an increased heart rate before a major presentation. When an individual understands the physical response to stress, they can be aware of the purpose or reason behind the anxiety. Anxiety is there to help individuals prepare to handle threats or challenges in their lives. A student can learn to say to themselves, "I am experiencing anxiety because this is my body preparing me for something big. I have control over this emotion because I can reflect about its purpose and understand that this is my body's response to preparing me for the challenge before me."

+ Teach students to be aware of the thoughts that accompany emotions. If these thoughts can be identified, they can be evaluated and questioned. For example, some gifted students may simply need some "worry time" where they can state (or write down) the thoughts they have associated with their worry. For example, a gifted student might be worried about performing well at a competition. You can guide the student to reflect, "This would be a terrible thing because . . ." and then from this response, prompt the student to think, "This would be a terrible thing because . . ." When these fears are articulated, the root cause of anxiety may come to surface. The process helps a student unravel complexities related to the emotion and develop self-awareness. When individuals have self-awareness about their lives, they have more control over their lives and how they navigate their environment.

+ Encourage students to practice a number of anxiety management strategies, including deep breathing, progressive muscle relaxation, mindfulness coloring, listening to relaxing music, and exercising.

Note. Adapted from *Teaching Tenacity, Resilience, and a Drive for Excellence: Lessons for Social-Emotional Learning for Grades 4–8,* by E. Mofield and M. Parker Peters, 2018, Prufrock Press.

gies. By striving to truly see, understand, and value the strengths of gifted learners, the team can uncover hidden potential, unleashing what's possible in the students' future talent trajectories. Ultimately, you want gifted students to know and appreciate their own strengths and see themselves as individuals of potential. Through collaborative consultation, you have the opportunity to advocate for gifted learners by sharing how giftedness intersects with achievement through factors such as learning differences, attention, motivation, and social-emotional issues, so that students can thrive in their learning and future pursuits.

Chapter 10

Collaborating to Support Gifted Students From Diverse Backgrounds

This chapter focuses on how educators can collaborate to identify and support the development of the gifts and talents of students from diverse backgrounds. Like the previous chapter, many of the strategies in this section are foundational to collaboration efforts aimed at serving students directly or indirectly. The information here may be shared with an ESL specialist, classroom teacher, administrator, instructional coach, school psychologists, and others involved in the student's education, all in efforts to promote access to challenging curriculum.

Successful collaboration is dependent on efficient systems. As gifted programs work with other programs such as ESL programs, the focused efforts should address the spectrum of needs that might not be addressed within gifted services alone, with an aim to build structures for fluid services and support. Collaborative teams must consider how to remove barriers that many gifted students from diverse populations encounter in classrooms. This includes myths and misconceptions about these special populations, particularly how giftedness is perceived.

In the role of a gifted education teacher, it is essential to advocate for identifying and serving students from culturally, linguistically, and economically diverse (CLED) backgrounds. Collaboration may involve being part of a strategic planning team that aims to revise programs so they include equitable identification practices and services with supports for students, even beyond what they need in gifted education programs. Collaboration with classroom teachers, teams, and/or other specialists ultimately focus on the goal of facilitating differentiation that allows "access to rigorous content and addresses the cultural differences of their prior experiences" (Krugman & Iza, 2014, p. 128). In the sections that follow, we offer ways to advocate for and support these populations.

Identifying Gifted Students From Diverse Backgrounds

In collaboration efforts, it is of utmost importance to build the awareness among various stakeholders (i.e., administrators, teachers, board members, parents) that gifted students are indeed found from various backgrounds and cultures. Although the topic of identifying underrepresented populations is beyond the scope of this text, it is important to consider equitable practices in identification, including the use of universal screening, local norms, and multiple measures for identification (Plucker & Peters, 2018).

You may share screening tools with classroom teachers, such as the Talents, Abilities, and Behaviors (TABs) observation form (Frasier et al., 1995) or other observation measures. Classroom teachers can use the tool to assess every student in their class on basic attributes of giftedness (e.g., interests, motivation, humor, problem solving, etc.). These 10 attributes of giftedness on the TABs form may be seen in students regardless of socioeconomic status, culture, or race. Classroom-based collaboration may pave the way for a classroom teacher to observe these attributes during Scout Teaching while the gifted education teacher uses strategies that provide opportunities for students to demonstrate their talents.

We emphasize the need to address myths and misconceptions related to what giftedness looks like among various populations. For example, the characteristic of curiosity is often observed as students asking numerous questions, expressing themselves well, and being curious about how things work. However, in other cultures, asking a number of questions to an authority figure may be considered rude, and some students may not have the language to demonstrate their curiosity through questioning. Demonstrating creativity and problem solving may be seen through solving real-world individual problems (e.g., determining the best route home from school through several bus transfers). Students from diverse backgrounds may express creative elaboration in the casual register (through conversational styles, use of slang, etc.), communicating through story and/or symbol (Gay, 2002). Additionally, the characteristic of task commitment (persistence on a task over time) may not necessarily be displayed in academic work, but in work that is relevant to the child's own priorities and interests, such as persisting in sports or other activities valued by the community or family.

One approach to provide for the needs of students from diverse backgrounds, including students impacted by poverty, is front-loading, defined as:

> the process of preparing students for advanced content and creative and critical thinking prior to the formal identification process or before advanced-level courses are offered. The process of front-loading bridges the gap in the readiness of some CLED students, nurtures their abilities, and prepares them for success in advanced content programs. (Briggs et al., 2008, p. 137)

In the context of collaboration, this can involve working with a strategic team to develop other inclusive talent development program options, such as enrichment or collaborating with classroom teachers to explicitly teach critical and creative thinking applied to content. Overall, this is an opportunity in which students who might otherwise have limited access to talent development can interact with more advanced resources and develop skills that prepare them for more challenging work.

Bridging Access to Rigorous Content

Collaboration for students from CLED populations involves asking the question, "How can we support students where they are in order to access rigorous content?" Teachers can build on student strengths, experiences, and cultural background as a reference point of knowledge and skills. This creates "a strong bridge that will allow students to connect where they are to where they can be" (Slocomb et al., 2017, p. 129). Teachers must work from a strength-based perspective, focusing on the high ends of learning rather than basic low-end facts (Goings & Ford, 2018). When teachers work from a deficit-based model, students from diverse cultural backgrounds or poverty may never have the exposure or opportunity to engage in high-level learning experiences. During collaborative conversations, you can intentionally guide the conversation toward understanding student strengths as starting points for planning instruction.

While collaborating to address the needs of gifted students from CLED backgrounds, you can take what you know about differentiating for gifted learners and complement it with what you know about language development, culturally responsive instruction, and needs of students impacted by poverty. We must note that many of these practices and supports overlap for various underrepresented populations (i.e., students from poverty come from a variety of backgrounds, and

ELLs are not necessarily students from poverty). Figure 13 indicates the features of the Integrated Curriculum Model (VanTassel-Baska & Baska, 2019) as components for gifted curriculum (advanced content, advanced processes, and concepts, issues, and/or discipline generalizations). The figure also shows the supports needed to prepare students from various backgrounds in reaching the advanced content, process, and concept outcomes within a lesson. Throughout the sections that follow, these features are highlighted as instructional strategies that bridge gaps and remove barriers to help gifted learners access rigorous content.

The last row of Figure 13 shows that the bridge is supported by psychosocial and motivational scaffolding. For example, collaborative teams might consider ways to build psychosocial supports for eliminating stereotype threats by developing a sense of belongingness among gifted peers. Stereotype threat involves the awareness that being affiliated with a stereotyped group means being less competent or intelligent (Steele & Aronson, 1995). In order to combat the effects of stereotype threats, efforts should be made to promote high expectations of all students, and teachers may need to talk openly with marginalized students about stereotype threats and their effects (Good, 2012).

Although we have used the SCARF model (status, certainty, autonomy, relatedness, fairness; Rock, 2008) in this book as a foundation for thinking through enhancing relationships in professional collaboration, the same principles can be applied in establishing a sense of belonging among students from diverse backgrounds. For example, status is important, as students need to think and believe the teacher values their interests and cultural identity. Teachers must also be reminded that participating in advanced programming may be contrary to cultural expectations. These students might experience conflict of pursuing achievement versus affiliating with one's cultural expectations. For these reasons, educators must provide culturally responsive instruction that honors a student's cultural heritage and builds a psychological identity that "enables them to integrate multiple values and expectations with high academic achievement" (Olszewski-Kubilius & Clarenbach, 2012, p. 18). Along the lines of the other components of SCARF, students from diverse backgrounds also need a sense of certainty and predictability, as well as a sense of autonomy over how they learn. Building in structures of predictability can enhance the building of mental models for thinking through academic content. Autonomy is supported through opportunities to apply problem solving to real-world issues related to their own communities. Finally, relatedness and fairness are key factors in helping students feel that they (including their cultural identities) are respected and valued.

Other psychological supports include promoting a belief that abilities can grow from effort, preparing students in knowing how to deal with obstacles, explicitly teaching students to set goals and monitor progress toward these goals, and teaching appropriate coping skills to handle setbacks (Mofield & Parker Peters, 2018a).

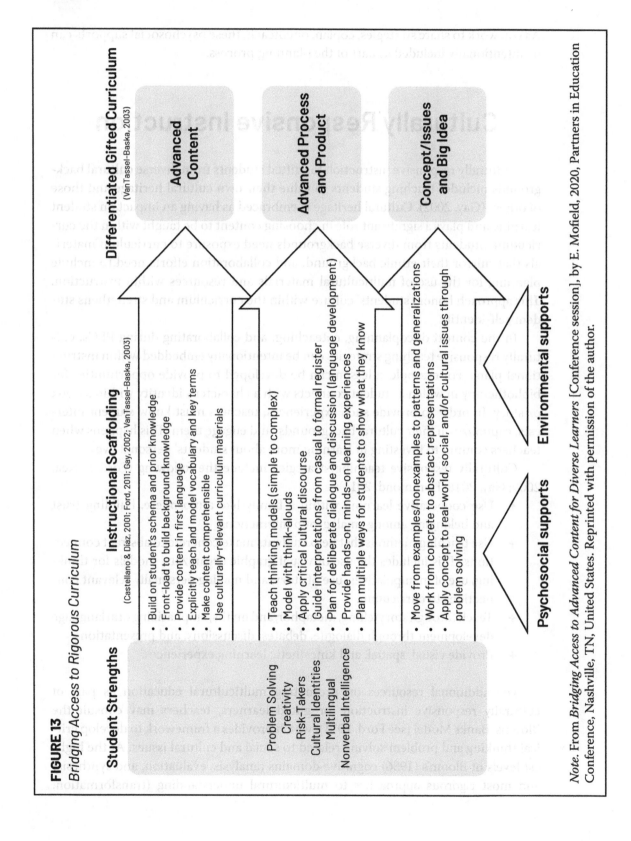

FIGURE 13
Bridging Access to Rigorous Curriculum

Student Strengths

- Problem Solving
- Creativity
- Risk-Takers
- Cultural Identities
- Multilingual
- Nonverbal Intelligence

Instructional Scaffolding
(Castellano & Díaz, 2001; Ford, 2011; Gay, 2002; VanTassel-Baska, 2003)

- Build on student's schema and prior knowledge
- Front-load to build background knowledge
- Provide content in first language
- Explicitly teach and model vocabulary and key terms
- Make content comprehensible
- Use culturally-relevant curriculum materials

- Teach thinking models (simple to complex)
- Model with think-alouds
- Apply critical cultural discourse
- Guide interpretations from casual to formal register
- Plan for deliberate dialogue and discussion (language development)
- Provide hands-on, minds-on learning experiences
- Plan multiple ways for students to show what they know

- Move from examples/nonexamples to patterns and generalizations
- Work from concrete to abstract representations
- Apply concept to real-world, social, and/or cultural issues through problem solving

Differentiated Gifted Curriculum
(VanTassel-Baska, 2003)

Advanced Content

Advanced Process and Product

Concept/Issues and Big Idea

Psychosocial supports   **Environmental supports**

Note. From *Bridging Access to Advanced Content for Diverse Learners* [Conference session], by E. Mofield, 2020, Partners in Education Conference, Nashville, TN, United States. Reprinted with permission of the author.

As you work to share strategies, coplan, or coteach, these psychosocial supports can be intentionally included as part of the planning process.

Culturally Responsive Instruction

Culturally responsive instruction for gifted students from diverse cultural backgrounds includes teaching students to value their own cultural heritage and those of others (Gay, 2002). Cultural heritage is embraced as having an impact on student learning and plays a significant role in choosing content to be taught within the curriculum. Students from diverse backgrounds need exposure to curriculum materials that mirror their ethnic background, and collaboration efforts need to include planning for the use of multicultural materials and resources within instruction. This approach honors students' culture within the curriculum and strengthens student self-identity.

In the context of coplanning, coteaching, and collaborating during PLCs, culturally responsive teaching strategies can be intentionally embedded within instructional plans. For example, a lesson can be developed to provide opportunities for bibliotherapy in which a student connects with a character's identity within a book or story. In order to provide such experiences, teachers must know student interests, capitalize on their cultural backgrounds, and engage them. This happens when teachers commit to investing in learning more about students' personal lives.

Culturally responsive teaching strategies include the following (Ford & Kea, 2009; Gay, 2018; Hammond, 2014):

+ Use cooperative learning within a family-like atmosphere, building trust and belonging among small group interactions.
+ Use teaching methods that help students make concrete to abstract connections. This includes the use of visual graphic organizers, models for thinking, use of manipulatives, use of story, and making personally relevant connections to curriculum.
+ Teach through storytelling, metaphor, and myths, emphasizing oral language development through dialogue, debates, discussions, and presentations.
+ Provide visual, spatial, and kinesthetic learning experiences.

For additional resources on promoting multicultural education as part of culturally responsive instruction for gifted learners, teachers may consult the Blooms-Banks Model (see Ford, 2011), which provides a framework to develop critical thinking and problem solving related to social and cultural issues. At the highest levels of Bloom's (1956) cognitive domains (analysis, evaluation, and synthesis) and most rigorous approaches to multicultural understanding (transformation, social action; Banks, 2009), tasks are designed to guide students to think critically, solve problems, and develop action plans related to multicultural issues and topics. This, in turn, provides opportunities for students to develop a sense of self-agency in which they can be aware of or actively address issues relevant to their lives. For example, for incorporating "social action" with the synthesis/create level of Bloom's taxonomy, students may create a service announcement about an important issue in their school or community (e.g., cyberbullying) in order to promote change. To incorporate "transformation," which largely involves perspective-taking with Bloom's evaluation level, students may determine who has power and who does not have power in a story, and offer insight into the character's thoughts, motives, and action through that character's perspective. As you coplan or coteach with classroom teachers, this model can be especially helpful in planning vertically differentiated tasks with sophisticated critical thinking and problem solving applied to real-world issues. For example, the gifted education teacher and classroom teacher might coplan for Tiered Teaching using the Blooms-Banks Model as a way to engage students in developing action plans for relevant issues their lives.

Gifted English Language Learners

English language learners are often underrepresented in gifted education programming. There is a misconception that ELLs need a focus on remediation rather than developing their talents. Through collaborative efforts, gifted education teachers might advocate for addressing misconceptions about this population. First, educators should understand that how intelligent a person is has nothing to do with the language they speak. If ELLs cannot speak fluent English, this is not necessarily a reflection of a lack of ability. Unfortunately, some individuals may have an implicit bias in thinking that intelligence equates to how proficiently a student can speak one language (Matthews & Castellano, 2014).

When considering characteristics of giftedness, it may be more difficult for teachers to recognize a number of gifted behaviors, such as curiosity, because when ELLs are learning English, they may be quieter than other students, refraining from asking the teacher as many questions in English as other typical gifted students. As mentioned previously, in some cultures, it is perceived as inappropriate to ask too many questions when interacting with an authority figure, such as a teacher.

There is also often a misconception that gifted students make good grades, excel in multiple academic areas, and display good school behaviors. Such misconceptions about giftedness also impact ELLs, for these students may not necessarily make good grades or have strengths in all academic areas. Grades may not reflect actual aptitude, as grades are often reflective of language proficiency (Matthews,

2014). ELLs need to have ways to show what they know in unique ways through varied types of products (e.g., beyond written text, use of visual or media representations). For example, performance on extended projects is more likely to demonstrate student understanding of content rather than assignments or tasks that are narrowly focused on writing.

Identifying and Serving Gifted ELLs

As you advocate for identifying and serving gifted ELLs while working with classroom teachers and administrators, you can provide awareness regarding the strengths often noted of this population. For example, as explained by Matthews and Castellano (2014), because ELLs are learning and playing with a new language and are eager to learn and excel in the new language, they naturally take more risks in their learning. Additionally, they are able to pay attention for up to 20% longer than typical students and often show higher levels of intrinsic motivation compared to other students.

Through collaboration with classroom teachers and ESL teachers, you can share characteristics of gifted ELLs, as well as instructional approaches for supporting them (see Table 28). Applying these instructional supports during Scout and Stretch coteaching can also be an effective way to identify ELLs who should be considered for formal gifted identification.

Collaboration between the ESL teacher, gifted education teacher, and classroom teacher brings diverse areas of expertise for supporting ELLs. All collaborators have an opportunity for improved teaching by learning specialized approaches that maximize student success. For example, the ESL teacher can share elements of sheltered instruction (e.g., design content-driven instruction, make content accessible, foster language use; Echevarría & Graves, 2015) and differentiation methods to meet the student's language needs. Collaboratively, lessons can be developed to provide multiple means of representation, engagement, and expression (see http://www.cast.org) so that ELLs can access advanced curriculum.

Many best practices for use with ELLs can be found within the Coaching Tool for Classrooms Supporting Gifted Education (Montgomery, 2001; see Table 29). Together, gifted education teachers, instructional coaches, ESL teachers, and classroom teachers can use this tool to reflect upon, inform, and plan for teaching gifted students from diverse populations. This resource might serve as a foundation for collaborative teams to work together to promote learning environments that support CLED gifted students by providing exemplary features for the physical environment, classroom interactions, curriculum, and assessment practices. Additionally, it may serve as a third point coaching tool as discussed in Chapter 8.

TABLE 28
Characteristics of Gifted ELLs and Instructional Approaches

Characteristics of Gifted ELLs	Instructional Approaches
+ Have high ability in math reasoning (because this is not as language-based as other content areas). + Have a deep interest in a topic. + Communicate complex reasoning through symbol or analogy. + Learn things quickly. + Acquire new language quickly. + Translate quickly and/or at an advanced level. + Code switch easily (think in both languages with ease). + Extend knowledge to new applications. + Are self-starters; have enhanced intrinsic motivation. + Respond quickly to front-loading exposure in enrichment; demonstrate or quickly develop skills when given opportunities to problem solve and apply critical thinking.	+ Use a gradual release model: Teach a new concept, provide contexts for students to practice the skill, and apply the new learning. The direct "I do, we do, you do" approach can be especially beneficial. + Instead of focusing on remediation, allow the students to demonstrate what they know and what they can do. + Allow students to work in pairs and with many opportunities for verbal interactions. Opportunities to communicate must be deliberately planned so that language communication skills can develop. + Use service-learning to engage gifted ELLs in developing critical thinking, language skills, and problem-solving skills. + Provide lessons that move learning from concrete to abstract, building from their personal lives and backgrounds as starting points. + Provide opportunities to speak and read in first language in order to access rigorous curriculum.

Note. Adapted from Matthews and Castellano, 2014; National Center for Research in Gifted Education, 2016.

Supporting Academic Language

ELLs benefit from instructional scaffolds for processing and producing language. One type of scaffold is the use of sentence frames. In Figure 14, sentence frames are provided for supporting reasoning in academic discourse. Additionally, these can serve as think-aloud prompts teachers can use when modeling how to think about and reason through academic content. To build from concrete to abstract thinking, students need explicit models for thinking (e.g., graphic organizer of Paul and Elder's [2019] elements of reasoning, etc.), including exposure to listening to structures of academic discourse associated with these models.

Sentence frames can give students confidence in starting conversations with their peers. Also, they allow students to use their cognitive effort on learning the

TABLE 29
Coaching Tool for Classrooms Supporting Gifted Education

"How to create and effectively support an inclusive, culturally-rich gifted education classroom environment that meaningfully respects and honors the diversity of all learners"

This *Coaching Tool for Classrooms Supporting Gifted Education* was created by a collaborative working group of gifted education experts representing state, district, and school administrators, classroom teachers, and university faculty, and was supported through the Washington Elementary School District's Project Bright Horizon Jacob K. Javits Gifted & Talented Education Grant program, and Project REGALOS Title III gifted education grant program. It is intended to be a representative reflection of current evidenced-based exemplary and promising practices with respect to providing classroom services for culturally and linguistically diverse gifted student populations.

Building and district administrators, site coordinators and program coaches may utilize this tool to support their diverse gifted education programs. It may also be used to assist classroom teachers to effectively reflect upon, and inform, their own classroom practices. The primary goal of this tool is to foster and support a culture of high expectations and program standards for diverse gifted education classrooms and to achieve the following outcomes:

Outcomes for Administrators:	Outcomes for Teachers:	Outcomes for Students and Families:
+ Enable administrators to become more effective instructional leaders to support diverse gifted education programs on their campus + Ensure classrooms are responsive to the unique needs of diverse gifted learners	+ Ensure classrooms are responsive to the unique needs of diverse gifted learners + Guide and inform teachers on how to effectively provide curriculum and instruction, and implement assessment practices in a classroom of diverse gifted learners	+ Ensure a positive classroom environment that values and honors each student's unique learning style and cultural and linguistic background, and provides opportunities to grow academically, cognitively, socially, and emotionally according to their abilities and talents

This tool was not designed or intended for use as a formal program assessment, but rather as a coaching tool to assist classroom teachers to become more effective educators of their culturally and linguistically diverse gifted learners—and to help administrators to become more effective instructional leaders in supporting diverse gifted education programs on their campuses.

TABLE 29, *continued*

For more information, please contact:

Peter C. Laing
Project Director

Project Bright Horizon
Jacob K. Javits Gifted & Talented Education Grant Program
Washington Elementary School District
4650 West Sweetwater
Glendale, Arizona 85304
Phone: (602) 347-2644
Fax: (602) 346-2683
Email: plaing@wesd.k12.az.us

Coaching Tool for Classrooms Supporting Gifted Education Development Team:

Dr. Jaime Castellano, Consultant—*Project Bright Horizon, Washington Elementary School District*

Peter C. Laing, Project Director—*Project Bright Horizon, Washington Elementary School District*

Andree Charlson, Principal—*Washington Elementary School District*

Barbara Post, Administrator for Gifted Services—*Washington Elementary School District*

Jeff Hipskind, Director of Gifted Education—*Arizona Department of Education*

Laura Anderson, Director of Gifted Education—*Paradise Valley Unified School District*

Dr. Dina Brulles, Director of Gifted Education—*Glendale Elementary School District*

Kim Landsdowne, Director of Gifted Education—*Scottsdale Unified School District*

Sue Goltz, Principal—*Madison Elementary School District*

Heidi Cocco, Teacher of the Gifted—*Paradise Valley Unified School District*

Physical Environment			3: Clear and Convincing Evidence 2: Somewhat Evident 1: Not Evident
3	2	1	Flexible organization of classroom space and furniture to create an inviting atmosphere and positive environment that accommodates diverse teaching and learning styles
3	2	1	Extensive visuals supporting specific, relevant academic and affective learning and language acquisition objectives (i.e., relevant, current bulletin boards having a multicultural focus)
3	2	1	Learning and language objectives are written in comprehensible student language and clearly displayed in the classroom
3	2	1	Student products representative of current language acquisition and content area standards and objectives, and that reflect the use of critical thinking processes, are prominently displayed
3	2	1	Integrated use of technology and multimedia resources to authentically facilitate student instruction and enhance learning
3	2	1	A literature corner incorporating a variety of interesting, culturally diverse reading materials and resources, addressing a wide range of reading levels and abilities
3	2	1	A supply center readily accessible to children that incorporates a broad range of diverse user-friendly materials and resources to encourage, engage, and support creative thinking activities

TABLE 29, *continued*

Classroom Interactions   3: Clear and Convincing Evidence   2: Somewhat Evident   1: Not Evident

Student to Student				Teacher to Student				Student to Content			
Mutual respect of cultural and linguistic diversity of peers	3	2	1	Respectful of the cultural and linguistic diversity of all students	3	2	1	Quality student products of appropriate complexity, depth and breadth	3	2	1
Respectful of the diverse ability levels of peers	3	2	1	Clear, high expectations of performance and positive reinforcement	3	2	1	Active participation, allows for experimental, hands-on, discovery learning	3	2	1
Supportive, positive reinforcement	3	2	1	Encourages divergent, critical and creative thinking	3	2	1	Engages students at the higher levels of Bloom's taxonomy	3	2	1
Active cooperative learning groups	3	2	1	Shared inquiry, Socratic and higher-level questioning techniques	3	2	1	Allows for acceleration where appropriate	3	2	1
Flexible grouping strategies	3	2	1	Use of guided and informal group discussions	3	2	1	Provides opportunities for independent study, research, and extended learning	3	2	1
Active listening to build upon and refine ideas and concepts	3	2	1	Effective use of accountable talk	3	2	1	Use of effective time-management strategies	3	2	1
Frequent opportunities for academic linguistic interaction, to build and accelerate CALP (*Cognitive Academic Language Proficiency*)	3	2	1	Guides and facilitates instruction, allowing for student exploration, discovery, and growth	3	2	1	Appropriate use of graphic organizers	3	2	1
Opportunities to demonstrate and build leadership and character	3	2	1	Engages and informs parents regarding the academic growth of their child	3	2	1	Utilizes effective note-taking strategies to independently facilitate their own learning	3	2	1
Student Metacognition				**Student Metacognition**							
Active sharing, describing, and feedback regarding thinking strategies individual students use to solve problems	3	2	1	Models task-specific effective reflective thinking processes and strategies (planning, reflecting, and evaluating)	3	2	1	Encourages ongoing self-reflection, evaluation, and feedback on how their thinking strategies impact learning	3	2	1

TABLE 29, *continued*

Curriculum Instruction	3: Clear and Convincing Evidence	2: Somewhat Evident	1: Not Evident
Students are able to see themselves reflected in the curriculum materials used in the classroom	3	2	1
Instructional methods of delivering the curriculum actively integrate strategies that provide for the accelerated development of CALP (*Cognitive Academic Language Proficiency*)	3	2	1
Differentiated according to individual ability and need, allowing for growth, increased depth and breadth and acceleration as appropriate	3	2	1
Incorporates objectives for affective and personal development and growth and exploring heritage culture	3	2	1
Designed to reflect higher levels of Bloom's taxonomy	3	2	1
Instructional strategies that promote critical and creative thinking, to include flexible grouping, higher level questioning, compacting, tiered assignments, scaffolding, interdisciplinary thematic units, and open-ended projects	3	2	1

Assessment Practices	3: Clear and Convincing Evidence	2: Somewhat Evident	1: Not Evident
Performance-based assessment options are available and appropriately utilized	3	2	1
Appropriately considers the cultural, ethnic, linguistic, and socioeconomic diversity of the students assessed	3	2	1
Assessment practices and options are transparent, with clearly stated teaching objectives and aligned outcomes, and students are aware of the specific expectations and criteria for assessment	3	2	1
Students are evaluated and assessed on content knowledge only—*not* on level of language proficiency	3	2	1
Flexible and adaptable to diverse learning styles of students, and incorporates both structured (observations, conferences, interviews) and unstructured assessment practices (journals, portfolios, storytelling, games, groups, technology), and allows for self-assessment, peer assessment, and student developed rubrics for assessment	3	2	1
Effectively assesses higher order thinking, critical and creative thinking, and problem solving	3	2	1
Assessment data are used to authentically inform instructional practices	3	2	1
Effectively builds upon and gauges prior knowledge through the use of frequent preassessment	3	2	1
Students are assessed using grade-level standards	3	2	1
Assessment practices are used to accommodate and strengthen student's CALP (*Cognitive Academic Language Proficiency*) level	3	2	1
Divergent solutions, when substantiated by students, are accepted and supported	3	2	1
Parents, as practicable, are informed of assessment results in their heritage language	3	2	1

Note. Adapted from *Project Bright Horizon*, by Washington Elementary School District, n.d., https://www.azed.gov/gifted-education/project-bright-horizon.

FIGURE 14

Sentence Frames for Reasoning

The reason I think this is because _____ .

If we know this _____ then we can figure out _____ .

I question the credibility of _____ because _____ .

I am going to argue _____ because _____ .

Some might see this differently, though. Some might argue that _____ .

The positive things about this are _____ , the negative things are _____ .

This might lead to _____ which might lead to _____ .

There's a fine line, though, between _____ and _____ .

Note. From *Bridging Access to Advanced Content for Diverse Learners* [Conference session], by E. Mofield, 2020, Partners in Education Conference, Nashville, TN, United States. Reprinted with permission of the author.

---

content rather than how to phrase something correctly. Depending on their level of proficiency, students may need additional support, such as a word bank along with the sentence frames. As students progress in their learning, they can rely less on these types of support. Resource 12 provides frames for supporting the stretch prompts presented in Chapter 6. These frames can support a variety of students (e.g., young students, twice-exceptional students, students impacted by poverty) in producing responses for high-level thinking.

With appropriate scaffolds, high-potential ELLs can engage in high-level thinking before becoming proficient in their second language. Maintaining high expectations, providing opportunities for students to build on and adjust their schemas, and providing contexts that allow for students to actively process and use academic language will support the development of academic language. When coplanning differentiated instruction for this population, you can focus on building in activities for multiple verbal interactions through small-group discussions, debates, jigsaws, and think-pair-share dialogue. Ultimately, if academic language is not practiced, it is not developed (Anderson, 2015).

The World-Class Instruction, Design, and Assessment (WIDA Consortium, 2014) English Learning Development (ELD) standards provide guidance for teachers to make strategic decisions on planning supports for ELLs in speaking, writing, reading, and listening. ELLs range in levels of language performance. The WIDA ELD model performance indicators allow teachers to understand language progression and the types of supports needed to guide students to the next level by providing flexible examples and guidance on the following:

+ What language are the students expected to process or produce at each level of proficiency?

**What are the parts of ____ ?
What is the overall structure?**

The parts include ____ .

The big part of the structure is ____ made up of the smaller parts, such as ____ .

____ changes the structure.

ANALYSIS

How do the parts relate to one another? What happens if a part is removed?

____ influences ____ .

____ relates to ____ .

____ changes ____ .

If ____ is removed, then ____ .

What are the causes and effects of the problem/issue?

____ , ____ , and ____ cause the problem.

The effects of the problem are ____ , ____ , and ____ .

PROBLEM-SOLVING

What do we not know about the problem? What do we need to know in order to make a plan?

We do not know ____ about the problem. We would need to know ____ in order to make a plan.

List what you know about the topic. Choose a thing or place. List things about the thing or place.

Topic	Thing/Place
1.	1.
2.	2.
3.	3.
4.	4.
5.	5.

METAPHORICAL THINKING

Make connections to show how the topic is like the thing or place.

____ is like ____ because ____ .

____ is like ____ because ____ .

What decisions need to be made about _____ ?

CRITICAL THINKING

We need to decide:
If _____
What _____
How _____

What criteria can we use to make our decision?

We will ask:
Is it _____ ?
Does it _____ ?

What was most difficult to do or understand?

METACOGNITION

The most difficult part to understand was _____ .

What skills do I need in moving forward? What do I do next?

I still need _____ .

Next, I will _____ .

What connections can you make with this topic to your own life or other content we have learned?

TRANSFER

This is like _____ because _____ .

This relates to _____ because _____ .

How does an expert think about this topic? How does an expert apply this thinking to real-world contexts?

An expert such as a _____ might study more about _____ .

An expert might ask _____ .

An expert may use this to _____ .

Create a debatable question for the topic.

DEBATE

Should _____ ?

Is _____ or _____ better?

Is it right that _____ ?

Agree or disagree: _____

What are various perspectives of the debate? What evidence supports these perspectives?

_____ would think _____ because _____ .

Note. Created by E. Mofield.

+ Which language functions reflect the cognitive function at each level of proficiency?
+ Which instructional supports (sensory, graphic, and interactive) are necessary for students to access content? (WIDA Consortium, 2014, p. 13)

WIDA scores provide language proficiency levels that can be associated with "Can Do Descriptors" to signify what a student can do at that level. The goal then is to support a student to move to the next level of proficiency. In addition, the model performance indicators provide examples of how students use language across varying proficiency levels. For example, the cognitive function of "analyze" varies from label drawing (Level 1—entering), describe in detail (Level 3—developing), to reproduce stories (Level 5—bridging). The indicators provide examples of supports across various contexts and levels ranging from word banks, visuals, and sentence frames to less structured sentence frames. These standards can be especially useful in collaborating with ESL or classroom teachers in planning supports for students interacting with advanced content.

Gifted Students Impacted by Poverty

While working with other school personnel, you have an important role to advocate for identification of underrepresented populations of gifted learners, including gifted students impacted by poverty. The gifts and talents of students from this population may go unnoticed without opportunities for all students to be exposed to high-level content, rigorous instruction, and high expectations. Too often, instruction for students from poverty may overly focus on building basic skills or remediating deficits. Because many students from poverty are overlooked as qualifying for gifted education, serving a broader population of students through a spectrum of services (including push-in with coteaching) can offer support and exposure to enrichment and deeper learning.

Additionally, and mentioned previously, the use of front-loading (providing early exposure to talent development opportunities, enrichment, and engagement with advanced curriculum before formal identification) can be an effective way to address readiness levels and prepare students for gifted/advanced programming before formal identification. For example, through Carousel Teaching, you may use a station activity that offers explicit teaching of critical thinking or creative thinking. As students are exposed to these thinking structures, this builds schemas for learning and processing more advanced content. Other coteaching structures such as Stretch and Scout Teaching with intentional front-loading can also pave the way to spot talent that may otherwise go unnoticed.

When consulting or coplanning instruction for gifted students from poverty, you must work from a strength-based perspective and use appropriate scaffolding to support students to engage with advanced content. Deficit thinking is based on the idea that students should be able to adjust to the school environment rather than the school environment responding to the needs of students (Goings & Ford, 2018). Deficit thinking assumes intellectual and motivational deficits are to blame for poor school performance rather than larger economic and sociopolitical systemic structures that perpetuate poverty and inequity. Ultimately, a strength-based perspective includes planning instruction around enhancing what students can do. To maintain a strength-based approach, you must be attuned to biases and assumptions held by yourself and other educators around deficit thinking. For example, it may be common to hear another teacher explain background factors that inhibit a student's success (e.g., student is from a one-parent home, substance abuse in the home, etc.), but you may redirect the conversation to focus on how the student might flourish in contexts that can be provided at school, emphasizing high expectations and offering ideas for scaffolding so that the student has an opportunity for his or her talents to be recognized and cultivated.

The instructional supports provided in Figure 15 can be useful as you work collaboratively with classroom teachers to coplan instruction. For example, you may consider planning for the integration of a concept idea, such as "change" or "power." Students may first think about how they see forms of power in their daily lives. They may consider concrete forms of power in relationships (seen in movies, seen in their own relationships) and different types of power (e.g., electricity, water, etc.) before connecting to abstract ideas, such as concluding that power is any source of influence (Slocumb et al., 2017). Students might also sketch ideas and symbols related to power examples they see in their own lives, thus providing the "base" a teacher can work from to help them find patterns in moving to broad generalizations and ideas of "power" explored throughout the unit. Using sketches to visually represent mental representations of ideas with opportunities to verbally explain the meaning of the sketch can also enhance a student's ability to make abstract concepts more concrete (Ramos, 2015).

Beyond collaboration with school personnel, consider collaborative opportunities with outside community resources or universities. Chapter 11 discusses a number of ways to develop mentorships, enrich classroom practice, and engage in policy work while advocating for this population.

FIGURE 15
Supports for Gifted Students Impacted by Poverty

+ Integrate students' home culture into school.
+ Provide direct teaching of reasoning and processing skills (e.g., sequencing and cause-effect skills).
+ Incorporate active, hands-on learning and problem-solving opportunities.
+ Use visuals and graphic organizers for classifying and displaying content.
+ Provide engagement with stories to connect ideas within and across content.
+ Provide direct teaching of academic vocabulary to develop schema and cognitive structures of reasoning (patterns, reasoning, examples, inferences) as well as structures for patterns of academic discourse.
+ Use inquiry strategies and opportunities to explore multiple points of view.
+ Teach for deep understanding and transferability.

Note. Adapted from Callahan, 2007; Jensen, 2013; VanTassel-Baska, 2018.

Fostering Strengths

Positive things can happen when teachers share the responsibility for student learning, collaboratively focusing on building access to curriculum that develops students' strengths. Overall, in addressing the needs of gifted students from diverse populations through collaboration, you must remember to develop instructional contexts that allow students to "show" their giftedness. This includes removing barriers and maximizing supports that build a bridge to access rigorous content.

Chapter 11

Collaboration Beyond
the School

Within the field of education, collaboration is typically focused at the school or district level, including a variety of classroom teachers, specialists, and administrators. This book would be remiss, however, without addressing other key collaborative partners, consisting of parents, advocacy groups, universities, and other various agencies. Extending collaboration beyond the walls of the school not only fosters the development of talent, but also presents unique opportunities not typically found within the school day to engage and challenge gifted learners. This chapter explains the importance of engaging in collaborative practice with those outside of the school system to expand opportunities for students to develop their gifts and talents.

Parents as Powerful Partners

In recognizing that parental involvement is a key factor in student success (Robinson et al., 2007), the first step in creating successful parental partnerships is to understand and address the types of questions and concerns they might have regarding their gifted child's education. Carpenter and Hayden (2018) outlined these areas as the following:

+ understanding the various roles of each person on the collaborative team and how they work together to create the most optimal learning environment for their child (e.g., school psychologist, gifted education teacher, administrator, classroom teacher, etc.);
+ learning the various strategies used to help meet their child's gifted needs (e.g., pretesting, curriculum compacting, grouping, acceleration, enrichment, etc.); and
+ being informed on the gifted identification policy and other services, as deemed appropriate, available to their child (e.g., counseling, special education supports, enrichment, acceleration, etc.).

Consistent communication (e.g., newsletters, emails, blogs, websites, etc.) also continues to strengthen these partnerships by informing parents what their child is learning and how it is being learned. This ongoing communication is important, needed, and valued, but it is not collaborative. Remember, collaboration is the action of working with someone to produce or create something, so in looking to expand collaborative practice with parents, you must explore the steps needed to progress from communication to collaboration.

Bridging From Communication to Collaboration

Consistent and ongoing communication with parents should start at the beginning of the school year. This might consist of a simple introductory letter that fosters responsive communication between you, the gifted education teacher, and the parents of your gifted students. As this first essential communication is drafted, think of words and phrases that can be integrated that elicit a feeling of camaraderie and collaboration. For instance, let parents know that you look forward to working *with* them throughout the year to enrich their child's educational experience, encourage them to reach out to you with any questions about the upcoming year, and invite them to share any special skills or specialized content knowledge they might be willing to share with the class if the opportunity presents itself. Continued communication through newsletters, blogs, or websites is essential.

While collaborating with parents, the TEAM frame is foundational to building relationships with those who may not have experience in education, those you may not see on a regular basis, and in many cases, those who have cultures and life experiences different than your own. Table 30 provides suggestions for fostering TEAM collaboration with parents.

TABLE 30
TEAMing With Parents

TEAM Attribute	Steps From Communication to Collaboration
Trust	+ Provide consistent, positive communication with parents using collaborative language, such as *work together*, *appreciate your feedback*, *team*, *partner*, *join*, etc. + Provide question stems for parents to ask their children after school based on the day's learning. This helps involve parents with their child's foundational learning. For instance, instead of a parent asking, "How was your day today?", parents would be able to ask, "I heard that you have been learning about recycling; what are some ideas you think we can try at home?" + Provide opportunities for parents to share feedback on their child's learning experiences.
Engage	+ Ask parents at the beginning of the year if they are interested in working with small groups or sharing special skills or knowledge with the whole class (to be developed through future collaboration). + Consider having a Parent Portal through which parents could contribute ideas and extensions on various learning activities, leading to future potential collaborative opportunities. + Seek out parents to share their expertise in developing a unit of study or participating as guest speakers.
Align	+ Be clear about the expectations of gifted programming in your building and explore how to work together if expectations are different. + Respect different cultures and life experiences by collaboratively developing a unit of study with parents to enrich and deepen a curricular focus. For example, during a unit on immigration, a collaborative opportunity might be coplanning to share the customs and traditions their families embrace as part of their cultural heritage.
Maintain	+ Engage in reflective practice after parents participate as guest speakers within the classroom. Together, the collaborative partners discuss the session and begin to brainstorm ideas for next steps, including possible follow-up questions, learning activities focused on thinking as a disciplinarian, and future collaborative opportunities. + Remain consistent with the TEAM frame throughout the year. This cannot be a "one and done" approach.

Preparing for Collaboration

Whether this takes the form of guest speakers, career day activities, or authentic classroom experiences, collaboration through parental partnerships can create real-world connections and provide exposure to specialists across different fields. To identify partnerships, consider using online surveys as valuable tools to recognize potential future collaborative opportunities. There are multiple free survey tools available, or you might consider using Google Forms to collect this information. If you work in an area where parents do not have access to technology, a paper survey is just as informative. Sample questions might focus on content expertise, occupations, skills, and/or special interests that parents would be willing to share to enrich classroom learning.

Promoting Positive Collaboration Addressing Individualized Learning Needs

The development of 504 or IEP plans presents an additional opportunity to collaborate with parents, in addition to the other educational professionals on the team. Whether the individualized plans are focused just on giftedness or also include twice-exceptional needs (see Chapter 9), there are times when emotions become involved in the collaborative process. If emotions impact collaboration to develop an individualized learning plan, focus on reaching a consensus, or opinion held by all or most. In doing so, stronger collaborative efforts will ensue.

In situations when emotions run high, take the time to consider the concerns that parents bring to the meeting. In many cases, parents are not familiar with the jargon that educators are so familiar with. In other scenarios, parents see their child struggling and feel unheard or judged. Parents might also have different levels of education, varying confidence levels, and various approaches to the collaborative process (Martin, 2005). In any of these cases, remain positive and continue to help bridge trust with parents. Table 31 provides suggestions for how to best address noncollaborative behaviors that might arise due to feelings of uncertainty. We refer to these as the four A's: absence, apathy, argument, and aggression (adapted from Martin, 2005). As discussed in Chapter 2, collaborative partnerships continue to be strengthened through positive intent, conveying the message that we believe others want to be responsible, competent, and involved.

Special considerations should be noted for collaborating with parents of ELLs. Representatives from all personnel involved in the child's services, including the gifted education teacher, ESL teacher, and classroom teacher, should be a part of a collaborative team. Krugman and Iza (2014) explained that this representation allows the parent to understand the integrated collaborative approach to the child's

TABLE 31
Proactive Approaches to Addressing Noncollaborative Behaviors

Noncollaborative Behavior	Proactive Approach to Collaboration
Absence: This behavior is signified by parents' nonattendance or nonparticipation in IEP and 504 meetings.	+ Communicate regularly with parents to let them know they are valued collaborative partners. + Let parents know that you value them as part of the collaborative team by asking them what date and time works best for their schedule *before* scheduling the meeting. + Encourage parents to participate via phone or virtual conference if they are unable to attend the meeting in person. + Ask for parental input prior to drafting the individualized learning plan (e.g., child's strengths, parental concerns, etc.). + Provide parents with a draft copy of the IEP or 504 prior to the meeting so they have time to process the information and feel involved in the process.
Apathy: With this behavior, parents might silently go along with the majority at the meeting, but secretly harbor resentment, mistrust, or disagreement.	+ Make it clear that the purpose of meeting is for all in attendance to work together to develop the individualized learning plan. + Encourage ongoing parental participation in the development of the individualized learning plan by asking for input or if they need any clarifying information. For instance, after sharing the student's current levels of performance, you might involve the parent by asking, "Are there other areas of Jordan's current performance that you would like to note within this section of the IEP? Your insights will help us work together to create more meaningful goals to help Jordan continue to grow in her learning." + Do *not* rush the meeting. Take the time to make sure the parents feel involved in the process. + Take a few minutes for all stakeholders to reflect at the end of the meeting about the decisions that were made.
Argument: This behavior consists of advancing and defending a conclusion that has already been reached. Parents may not continue to share ideas or be open to alternate viewpoints.	+ Begin meetings by celebrating the student's strengths and discuss how these strengths might be encouraged across different content areas and classroom rotations. + Let parents know they are heard by restating their concerns and connecting those concerns to an alternate situation. For example, "Thank you for collaborating with us on how to best help Jordan organize her thoughts during prewriting. In what ways can we help her communicate her need for support if she is ever unsure of what to do next?" + Provide concrete examples of how accommodations or modifications might look across different content areas (e.g., compacting for mastery of content in math and science, providing examples of note templates for different content areas, etc.). + Continue to use inclusive language (e.g., *we, together, our main focus*, etc.).

TABLE 31, *continued*

Noncollaborative Behavior	Proactive Approach to Collaboration
Aggression: This noncollaborative behavior is the most extreme, consisting of casting blame and raising voices. This behavior rarely becomes an issue if consistent communication and listening are implemented.	+ Focus on the child's strengths and address the child's challenges through those strengths. + Stay focused on helping the child move forward while addressing concerns. Do not focus on what is *not* working. + Allow parents the opportunity to finish sharing their thoughts. Do not interrupt, as this only intensifies hurt feelings. + Continue to communicate the importance of collaboration with all stakeholders prior to the meeting. + Be highly aware of your own body language (e.g., rolling eyes, looking at phone, crossing arms, tapping fingers, etc.). Sometimes it is not the words, but the actions of a person, that trigger aggression.

education in seeing how services connect and work together. It is less complicated for the parents when this happens in one meeting, rather than multiple meetings with various personnel. In addition, information should be communicated in the parent's heritage language by a fully bilingual interpreter. In collaborating with parents of ELLs, you can learn more about students' cultural experiences and capitalize upon them in instructional planning.

Parent Gifted Advocacy Groups

Often, parent advocates are the best catalysts for change in gifted education. Not only are they energetic, passionate volunteers who are committed to gifted education, but they also play a direct role in the election of local school board members, ask questions that challenge the status quo, anticipate future concerns, and actively seek out engagement in the educational process. In a sense, parents are the social capital that is often needed for change. McGee and Bowie (2011) explained that parent gifted advocacy groups also support gifted education by providing:

+ support to other parents of gifted children who quite often feel alone in raising children with exceptional abilities;
+ information about what giftedness means and how students can be best served;
+ social and cultural opportunities for gifted students to make new friends through event nights, outings, and special interest groups;
+ partnerships with PTOs to support gifted education within schools;

+ volunteers, funding, and supplies for gifted programming; and
+ newsletters and online resources on the needs of gifted learners.

Use these positive outcomes as potential ideas for future collaboration. Begin by determining if a parent gifted advocacy group is in your area. This can be done by checking with your school district or referencing https://www.hoagiesgifted.org, as it maintains a list of active parent advocacy groups based on location, both in the United States and abroad. If you find that your area has an active group, contact the group, and inquire how you might work together.

At the beginning stages of collaboration, the focus might be working together to coplan a presentation on key topics, such as perfectionism, underachievement, twice-exceptional learners, the college application process, or any other topic related to parents' interests. Once a strong collaborative practice is established, more involved efforts might be considered.

Potential collaboration might involve the following:

+ Sponsor a Saturday experience for students. This might include something as simple as a social game day when everyone brings their favorite games, to a more in-depth collaboration to host a competition, such as a math, science, or linguistic Olympiad.
+ Develop professional learning sessions to teach parents, educators, and community members about the characteristics and needs of gifted learners. These sessions could be presented at school, conference, or community meetings.
+ Design, create, and maintain a website to support gifted families.
+ Engage in fundraising efforts to raise money and awareness for gifted programming.

Regardless of the collaborative action, continue to be mindful of presuming positive intent throughout all communication efforts. In doing so, collaborative partners will feel more empowered, leading to greater potential for future collaborations, and an increase in parent involvement.

Community Collaboration

Collaboration with community partnerships can support gifted learners' academic needs, provide opportunities to cultivate their talents, and connect students with experts in the field. These partnerships can provide students exposure to a variety of content areas and support learning through a specific discipline.

As a gifted education teacher, you may collaborate to plan a lesson with a professional in the field. For example, through collaboration with an expert chemical engineer, together you might create a lesson in which the chemical engineer provides content-specific knowledge on the structures of chemical compounds and mixtures and how this applies to designing new products and materials. In this manner, experts in the field can share how their work directly relates to solving real-world problems. They can also share which resources, tools, models, or methods are needed to solve such problems. Through these experiences, students gain awareness for future career paths and models of inquiry in real-world contexts.

Identifying Potential Partnerships

Community partnerships might consist of corporations, libraries, park districts, and community colleges/universities, to name a few. One approach for identifying these future collaborative partners is to use community resources (e.g., newspapers, local bulletin boards, city hall, social media, etc.) to help locate community contacts. This might include searching for businesses in the area, reading local newspapers for stories about organizations and notables nearby, and contacting local government agencies and politicians.

Once the list of contacts is developed, reach out to initiate future collaborative partnerships. Seek out opportunities to cultivate and develop students' talent through partners who are open to provide mentoring, lead class demonstrations, lead workshops, judge events, provide shadowing opportunities, or share personal collections (e.g., historic artifacts, artwork, currency, insects, etc.).

Keeping Students as the Focus

All community partnerships should focus on developing the strengths and talents of students. As discussed in Chapter 3, educators must aim to understand student interests, areas of potential strengths, and value systems. For instance, if gifted students demonstrate strengths in math and spatial reasoning, seek out community partnerships that allow the opportunity to grow in fields of science, technology, engineering, chemistry, dentistry, and/or the visual arts. Likewise, for gifted students who excel in reading and writing, seek out potential mentorships in the humanities and social sciences (Park et al., 2007; Sorby et al., 2013; Stieff, 2013; Winner, 2009). While considering student strengths, do not forget to consider their hobbies as well as extracurricular interests. The culmination of this information will help determine which partnerships would be most beneficial for community collaboration.

Community Mentorships

Community-based mentorships offer an opportunity for sustained, ongoing collaboration. Mentor-mentee relationships allow students to learn from experts in the field who can provide ongoing support and coaching. In the context of talent development, the mentor is able to support the student in unique ways the teacher or school cannot by providing more one-on-one scaffolding for learning content-specific skills. Mentors can also provide personal emotional support and encouragement when the student is faced with a challenging task or setback (Knotek & Babinski, 2018). Gifted learners have shared that mentorships go beyond offering them the intellectual stimulation they enjoy to provide them with the emotional guidance, social skills, and vocational modeling that they value (Robinson et al., 2007).

Perhaps you are working to pair students with appropriate mentors. Table 32 provides the foundational groundwork needed to start and maintain successful mentorships, including key questions to ask the potential mentor during collaborative discussions. Overall, in line with the TEAM frame, clear expectations should be set to match goals to behavior expectations for both the mentor and mentee.

Community College and University Collaborative Opportunities

If you live in an area near a community college or local university, check to see if they offer programs to support gifted programming. These university-based programs often provide Saturday sessions, summer camps, and/or ongoing coursework that provide gifted students and their families additional learning experiences outside of the classroom. If you do not reside near this community resource, there are still many opportunities for gifted learners to access online programming focused on advanced content, specialized interests, and college-level courses through university outreach programs.

Although several of these options do not present opportunities for direct collaborative practice, they do serve as a meaningful resource for reaching out to highly qualified professionals. Consider contacting professors to serve as mentors or to enrich classroom instruction by being guest speakers, conducting experiments, or providing university-based field trips to experience learning through a specialized lab, simulator, or other university-based specialization. Such programs allow students to learn how experts approach their work in authentic ways, guiding their pursuits along similar paths.

TABLE 32
Foundational Groundwork for Successful Mentorships

Foundational Groundwork for Successful Mentorships	Guiding Collaborative Questions *(to the Mentor)*
Prepare the Student: During the initial stages of collaboration, share your insights of the student's abilities with the mentor. Quite often, those working as mentors do not have experience interacting with gifted students, resulting in trying to communicate with students in the same manner they would with adult colleagues. This can lead to potential frustrations from both the mentor and the gifted student. To address this issue, help the mentor learn what to expect from the student, while also learning how to best prepare the student for a successful mentorship.	+ What basic skills would be most helpful for the student to enter the mentorship (e.g., basic computer skills, ability to effectively communicate in writing, knowledge of various art mediums, etc.)? + Which "field-specific" terms should I (gifted education teacher) help the student learn before entering into the mentorship? + How can I, as the gifted education teacher, help to support the initial stages of this mentorship?
Build Access to Content Expertise: A successful mentorship presents an opportunity for the gifted student to learn how to navigate a specific discipline. Work with the mentor to develop meaningful questions focused on accessing rigorous, expert-level content.	+ How might we help the student seek new challenges within this mentorship? + How might the student's ongoing level of understanding be assessed throughout the mentorship? + How might you model what you do as an expert in the field, in a situation where you do not know the answer?
Make Real-World Connections: Beyond accessing rigorous content, the mentorship should focus on helping the gifted student "think" as a content-area disciplinarian through authentic learning experiences. This means that when presented with a problem, the student should be able to successfully implement discipline-specific methods and tools to solve real-world problems. Brainstorm with the mentor how these real-world connections can be integrated into the mentorship.	+ In knowing the types of problems you encounter on a daily basis, how can we create similar authentic learning experiences within this mentorship? + As an expert in the field, how does your work contribute directly to your discipline and other fields, and how can this best be communicated to the student? + How can we work together to help the gifted student understand the contributions of this mentorship to our global world?

TABLE 32, *continued*

Foundational Groundwork for Successful Mentorships	Guiding Collaborative Questions *(to the Mentor)*
Teach Psychosocial Skills: Psychosocial skills are the mental and social skills needed to achieve long-term goals. The mentor should help the student recognize how to navigate setbacks, manage self-doubt or anxiety, employ a positive mindset towards challenges, productively collaborate with others, and advocate for personal ideas in the face of criticism. The mentor can emphasize self-reflection on these skills.	+ How might you share advice on how you handle criticism and setbacks? + How can we help the student self-reflect on their mindset towards effort and challenge? How might we promote self-reflection on the student's current mindset? + What advice might you share on managing emotions (e.g., anxiety, self-doubt) within competitive environments? + In what ways do you collaborate with other professionals and what skills are needed to do so successfully?
Address Organizational Skills: A successful mentorship needs to integrate goal setting, time management, and organizational skills. Mentors can work to create experiences to support the gifted student in skills related to task management, setting priorities, record-keeping, and data collection specific to the specialty.	+ How do you manage ongoing tasks in your professional life, and how can we apply these strategies to the mentorship experience? + When we think of what projects we would like the mentee to work on through this mentorship, how might we break them into smaller steps to check progress and provide meaningful feedback? + How can we best support the student to maintain a sense of life balance throughout the mentorship process?

Local, State, and National Agencies

Local, state, and national gifted organizations serve as a valuable resource of professionals who advocate for gifted education and continually work to enhance the field of gifted education. In addition to providing recommendations, they also present future collaborative opportunities focused on creating meaningful professional learning for your school and expanding gifted advocacy in your area.

Professional Growth

We suggest working with your local, state, and/or national gifted organizations to find resources written by individuals involved in these groups. Quite often, these individuals are willing to collaborate on professional learning for your school or district. If they do not have the availability for ongoing collaboration, ask if they would be willing to participate in a virtual question-and-answer session related to their research or other publications. This collaborative effort directly connects teachers in the district with knowledgeable experts in the field and supports ongoing professional learning.

In addition to collaborating with individuals within these organizations, these various agencies also provide new avenues for your own continued professional growth and reflective practice. As you become involved, take the time to learn about the different collaborative opportunities within the organization. These might consist of serving on various committees, developing outreach efforts, or hosting events. Regardless of the manner of involvement, continue to seek out opportunities to expand your own professional practice and seek to make contributions in the field.

Gifted Advocacy

Local, state, and national agencies offer additional collaborative opportunities to advocate for resources, support, and funding for gifted education. By working alongside these groups, a greater awareness for the needs of gifted learners is made, leading to positive outcomes that benefit not only the gifted students, but also their families and the community as a whole (Roberts, 2017). These collaborative efforts continue to impact the laws and regulations that dictate how gifted learners' needs are addressed during the school day. In recognizing the far-reaching effects of policy change, Roberts (2017) provided the following guiding principles to focus these collaborative discussions:

+ Clarity ensures that the plan has a clear directive.
+ Support information establishes a strong research-based foundation.
+ Specificity provides specific information to implement the program.
+ Inclusiveness addresses who is involved with the plan.

Beyond exploring the collaboration required for creating purposeful policy, also consider how collaboration can be used to create action plans to gain support and elicit change. This might include methods to encourage involvement in the organization, directives to disseminate information and raise awareness for critical topics, and procedures to contact legislators regarding policy support. The following are suggestions that support gifted advocacy in this manner:

+ Work with others to create a phone tree and scripts for calling local legislators, asking for support for gifted education.
+ Collaboratively draft letters that could be sent to different agencies, legislators, and prominent influencers to harness support for gifted education.
+ Create a committee to publish online newsletters regarding gifted education to raise awareness and update followers of gifted advocacy efforts.
+ Design a website that disseminates information, research, and volunteer opportunities focused on gifted advocacy.

Although these are just a few suggestions to initiate collaborative discussions regarding advocacy efforts, the idea is that even the small efforts of making phone calls and writing letters are valuable collaborative efforts. Ultimately, collaboration with the purpose of advocating for gifted learners is an ongoing process and should consistently focus on promoting access to challenging learning experiences and developing the strengths and talents of students.

Concluding Thoughts

As we reflect on our own collaboration in coauthoring this book, we can attest to the value of using the TEAM frame in our own partnered work. Trusting each other by following through on tasks and being willing to give and receive honest feedback, engaging each other's strengths from our own previous experiences in the field, aligning our beliefs and values to connect to the ultimate overall purpose of the book (without going off on too many tangents), and maintaining our relationship by continually checking in, seeking feedback, and reflecting together has paved the way for a powerful and rewarding endeavor. Like other collaborative work, this has involved revision of initial plans, challenging each other's assumptions as well as our own, seeing matters from different perspectives, and providing sincere support and encouragement to each other along the way.

In a process that involves vulnerability, we learned to lean on the foundation of trust established from the onset of our work. Collaboration in the real world is messy but so fulfilling. We have both benefited from "colaboring" the writing of this book together as thinking partners, and from this experience, we pass our constructed shared knowledge to you. It is our hope you also experience the power of effective collaboration, and in doing so, your students will soar to unknown heights.

References

Aguilar, E. (2013). *The art of coaching: Effective strategies for school transformation.* Wiley.

Anderson, E. F. (2015). Engaging and effective strategies for English language learners. In D. Sisk (Ed.), *Accelerating and extending literacy for diverse students* (pp. 66–83). Rowman & Littlefield.

Antony, M. M., & Swinson, R. P. (2009). *When perfect isn't good enough: Strategies for coping with perfectionism.* New Harbinger.

Assouline, S. G., Foley Nicpon, M., & Huber, D. H. (2006). The impact of vulnerabilities and strengths on the academic experiences of twice-exceptional students: A message to school counselors. *Professional School Counseling, 10*(1), 14–23. https://doi.org/10.5330/prsc.10.1.y0677616t5j15511

Assouline, S. G., Foley Nicpon, M., & Whiteman, C. (2010). Cognitive and psychosocial characteristics of gifted students with written language disability. *Gifted Child Quarterly, 54*(2), 102–115. https://doi.org/10.1177/0016986209355974

Assouline, S. G., & Whiteman, C. S. (2011). Twice-exceptionality: Implications for school psychologists in the post–IDEA 2004 era. *Journal of Applied School Psychology, 27*(4), 380–402. https://doi.org/10.1080/15377903.2011.616576

Bambrick-Santoyo, P. (2019). What you practice is what you value. *Educational Leadership, 77*(3), 44–49.

Banks, J. A. (2009). *Teaching strategies for ethnic studies* (8th ed.). Allyn & Bacon.

Baum, S., & Schader, R. (2018, November). *The power of strength-based, talent-focused learning for 2e students* [Conference session]. giftED 18, Fort Worth, TX, United States.

Baum, S. M., Renzulli, S., & Rizza, M. G. (2006). The twice-exceptional adolescents: Who are they? What do they need? In F. A. Dixon & S. M. Moon (Eds.), *The handbook of secondary gifted education* (2nd ed., pp. 155–184). Prufrock Press.

Bloom, B. (Ed.). (1956). *Taxonomy of educational objectives: The classification of educational goals. Handbook I: Cognitive domain.* Longmans Green.

Briggs, C. J., Reis, S. M., & Sullivan, E. E. (2008). A national view of promising programs and practices for culturally, linguistically, and ethnically diverse gifted and talented students. *Gifted Child Quarterly, 52*(2), 131–145. https://doi.org/10.1177/0016986208316037

Brulles, D., Peters, S. J., & Saunders, R. (2012). Schoolwide mathematics achievement within the gifted cluster grouping model. *Journal of Advanced Academics, 23*(3), 200–216. https://doi.org/10.1177/1932202X12451439

Bruner, J. S. (1973). Organization of early skilled action. *Child Development, 44*(1), 1–11 https://doi.org/10.2307/1127671

Burkman, A. (2012). Preparing novice teachers for success in elementary classrooms through professional development. *Delta Kappa Gamma Bulletin, 78*, 23–33.

Callahan, C. M. (2007). What can we learn from research about promising practices in developing the gifts and talents of low-income students? In J. VanTassel-Baska & T. Stambaugh (Eds.), *Overlooked gems: A national perspective on low-income promising learners. Conference proceedings from the National Leadership Conference on low-income promising learners.* National Association for Gifted Children.

Carpenter, A. Y., & Hayden, S. M. (2018). Roles in gifted education: A parent's guide. *Parenting for High Potential, 7*(3), 2–5.

Castellano, J. A., & Díaz, E. (2001). *Reaching new horizons: Gifted and talented education for culturally and linguistically diverse students.* Allyn & Bacon.

Costa, A. L, & Gamston, R. J. (2015). *Cognitive coaching: Developing self-directed leaders and learners* (3rd ed.). Rowman & Littlefield.

Cotabish, A., & Robinson, A. (2012). The effects of peer coaching on the evaluation knowledge, skills, and concerns of gifted program administrators. *Gifted Child Quarterly, 62*(3), 160–170. https://doi.org/10.1177/0016986212446861

Covey, S. (2015). *The 7 habits of highly effective people.* Free Press. (Original work published 1989)

Danielson, C. (2008). *The handbook for enhancing professional practice using the framework teaching in your school.* ASCD.

de Bono, E. (2016). *Six thinking hats.* Penguin. (Original work published 1985)

Delisle, J. R. (2018). *Doing poorly on purpose: Strategies to reverse underachievement and respect student dignity.* ASCD.

DeWitt, P. (2017, January 25). *Which coaching is best for you?* Education Week. http://blogs.edweek.org/edweek/finding_common_ground/2017/01/which_coaching_is_best_for_you.html

Doubet, K. J., & Hockett, J. A. (2015). *Differentiation in middle and high school: Strategies to engage all learners.* ASCD.

DuFour, R., DuFour, R., Eaker, R., & Many, T. (2010). *Learning by doing: A handbook for professional learning communities at work* (2nd ed.). Solution Tree Press.

Eberle, B. (2008). *Scamper: Creative games and activities for imagination development.* Prufrock Press.

Echevarría, J., & Graves, A. (2015). *Sheltered content instruction: Teaching English learners with diverse abilities* (5th ed.). Pearson.

Every Student Succeeds Act, 20 U.S.C. § 6301 (2015). https://congress.gov/114/plaws/publ95/PLAW-114publ95.pdf

Feldman, K. (2016). *Actionable feedback for teachers: The missing element in school improvement.* Minnesota Association of School Administrators. https://www.mnasa.org/cms/lib6/MN07001305/Centricity/Domain/44/Feldman%20Actionable%20Feedback%20for%20Teachers.pdf

Fogarty, E. A., & Tschida, C. M. (2018). Using coteaching as a model of professional learning. In A. M. Novak & C. L. Weber (Eds.), *Best practices in professional learning and teacher preparation: Methods and strategies for gifted professional development* (Vol. 1, pp. 151–172). Prufrock Press.

Foley Nicpon, M., Allmon, A., Sieck, B., & Stinson, R. D. (2011). Empirical investigation of twice-exceptionality: Where have we been and where are we going? *Gifted Child Quarterly, 55*(1), 3–17. https://doi.org/10.1177/0016986210382575

Ford, D. Y. (2011). *Multicultural gifted education* (2nd ed.). Prufrock Press.

Ford, D. Y., & Kea, C. D. (2009). Creating culturally-responsive instruction: For students' and teachers' sakes. *Focus on Exceptional Children, 41*(9), 1–16. https://doi.org/10.17161/fec.v41i9.6841

Frasier, M. M., Hunsaker, S. L., Lee, J., Finley, V. S., García, J. H., Martin, D., & Frank, E. (1995). *An exploratory study of the effectiveness of the staff development model and the research-based assessment plan in improving the identification of gifted economically disadvantaged students* (RM95224). University of Connecticut, The National Research Center on the Gifted and Talented.

Friend, M. (2016). *Co-teaching: Creating success for all learners. Supplemental materials for the workshop Council for exceptional children and the San Mateo County Office of Education.* https://www.cec.sped.org/~/media/Files/Professional%20Development/HTW/2016%20HTW/Handouts/MFriendPresentationSanMateo92416.pdf

Friend, M., & Cook, L. (2017). *Interactions: Collaboration skills for professionals* (8th ed.). Allyn & Bacon.

Friend, M., Cook, L., Hurley-Chamberlain, D., & Shamberger, C. (2010). Co-teaching: An illustration of the complexity of collaboration in special education. *Journal of Educational and Psychological Consultation, 20*(1), 9–27. https://doi.org/10.1080/10474410903535380

Fullan, M. (2001). *Leading in a culture of change.* https://www.csus.edu/indiv/j/jelinekd/edte%20227/fullanleadinginacultureofchange.pdf

Gay, G. (2002). Preparing for culturally responsive teaching. *Journal of Teacher Education, 53*(2), 106–116. https://doi.org/10.1177/0022487102053002003

Gay, G. (2018). *Culturally responsive teaching: Theory, research, and practice.* Teacher's College Press.

Gentry, M., & Mann, R. L. (2009). Total school cluster grouping: Model, research, and practice. In J. S. Renzulli, E. J. Gubbins, S. K. McMillen, R. D. Eckert, & C. A. Little (Eds.), *Systems and models for developing programs for the gifted and talented* (2nd ed., pp. 211–234). Prufrock Press.

Goings, R. B., & Ford, D. Y. (2018). Investigating the intersection of poverty and race in gifted education journals: A 15-year analysis. *Gifted Child Quarterly, 62*(1), 25–30. https://doi.org10.1177/0016986217737618

Good, C. (2012). Reformulating the talent equation: Implications for gifted students' sense of belonging and achievement. In R. F. Subotnik, A. Robinson, C. M. Callahan, & P. Johnson (Eds.), *Malleable minds: Translating insights from psychology and neuroscience to gifted education* (pp. 37–54). University of Connecticut, The National Research Center on the Gifted and Talented.

Gross Cheliotes, L. M., & Reilly, M. F. (2010). *Coaching conversations: Transforming your school one conversation at a time.* Corwin.

Guilford, J. P. (1986). *Creative talents: Their nature, uses and development.* Bearly.

Haberlin, S. (2016). Teaching in circles: Learning to harmonize as a co-teacher of gifted education. *The Qualitative Report, 21*(11), 2076–2087. https://nsuworks.nova.edu/tqr/vol21/iss11/5

Hammond, Z. (2014). *Culturally responsive teaching and the brain: Promoting authentic engagement and rigor among culturally and linguistically diverse students.* Corwin.

Heacox, D., & Cash, R. M. (2014). *Differentiation for gifted learners: Going beyond the basics.* Free Spirit.

Hertberg-Davis, H. (2009). Myth 7: Differentiation in the regular classroom is equivalent to gifted programs and is sufficient: Classroom teachers have the time, the skill, and the will to differentiate adequately. *Gifted Child Quarterly, 53*(4), 251–253. https://doi.org/10.1177/0016986209346927

Hubbard, R. (2009). Tinkering change vs. system change. *Phi Delta Kappa International, 90*(10), 745–747. https://doi.org/10.1177/003172170909001013

Hudson, P., & Glomb, N. (1997). If it takes two to tango, then why not teach both partners to dance? Collaboration instruction for all educators. *Journal of Learning Disabilities, 30*(4), 442–448. https://doi.org/10.1177/002221949703000411

Hughes, C. (2011). Twice-exceptional children: Twice the challenges, twice the joys. In J. A. Castellano & A. D. Frazier (Eds.), *Special populations in gifted education: Understanding our most able students from diverse backgrounds* (pp. 153–173). Prufrock Press.

Hughes, C. E., & Murawski, W. W. (2001). Lessons from another field: Applying coteaching strategies to gifted education. *Gifted Child Quarterly, 45*(3), 195–204. https://doi.org/10.1177/001698620104500304

Individuals With Disabilities Education Act, 20 U.S.C. §1401 *et seq.* (1990). https://sites.ed.gov/idea/statuteregulations

Jensen, E. (2013). *Engaging students with poverty in mind: Practical strategies for raising achievement.* ASCD.

Joyce, B. R., & Showers, B. (2002). *Student achievement through staff development* (3rd ed.). ASCD.

Juntune, J. (2013). *Differentiation of curriculum for gifted and talented students.* TAGT OnDemand. https://tagtondemand.com/product/differentiation-of-curriculum-and-instruction-for-the-gifted-and-talented-6-hour

Kane, J., & Henning, J. E. (2004). A case study of the collaboration in mathematics between a fourth-grade teacher and a talented and gifted coordinator. *Journal for the Education of the Gifted, 27*(4), 243–266. https://doi.org/10.4219/jeg-2004-318

Kaplan, S. (2009). Layering differentiated curricula for the gifted and talented. In F. A. Karnes & S. M. Bean (Eds.), *Methods and materials for teaching the gifted* (3rd ed., pp. 107–156). Prufrock Press.

Kee, K., Anderson, K., Dearing, V., Harris, E., & Shuster, F. (2010). *Results coaching: The new essentials for school leaders.* Corwin.

Knight, J. (2019). Why teacher autonomy is central to coaching success. *Educational Leadership, 77*(3), 14–20.

Knotek, S. E., & Babinski, L. M. (2018). Mentoring and developmentally productive environments. In P. Olszewski-Kubilius, R. F. Subotnik, & F. C. Worrell (Eds.), *Talent development as a framework for gifted education: Implications for best practices and applications in schools* (pp. 205–230). Prufrock Press.

Krugman, V. K., & Iza, L. (2014). Building collaborative partnerships in schools and communities. In M. Matthews & J. Castellano (Eds.), *Talent development for English language learners: Identifying and developing potential* (pp. 125–166). Prufrock Press.

Kruse, S. (1999). Collaborate. *Journal of Staff Development, 20*(3), 14–16.

Landrum, M. S. (2001). An evaluation of the catalyst program: Consultation and collaboration in gifted education. *Gifted Child Quarterly, 45*(2), 139-151. https://doi.org/10.1177/001698620104500207

Landrum, M. S. (2002). *Consultation in gifted education: Teachers working together to serve students.* Creative Learning Press.

Lenard, M., & Townsend, M. (2017). *Academically gifted co-teaching in the Wake County Public School System: Implementation, perceptions, and achievement* (DRA Report No. 17.03). https://webarchive.wcpss.net/results/reports/2017/1703aig-coteaching.pdf

Lencioni, P. (2003). Building a healthy organization. *School Administrator, 70*(2), 39–43.

Lewis, K. D., Novak, A. M., & Weber, C. L. (2018). Where are gifted students of color? *The Learning Professional, 39*(4), 50–53.

Lipton, L., & Wellman, B. (with Humbard, C.). (2001). *Mentoring matters: A practical guide to learning focused relationships.* Sherman.

Martin, N. R. M. (2005). *A guide to collaboration for IEP teams.* P. H. Brookes.

Masso, G. (2004, Summer). Co-teaching in a differentiated classroom: The impacts on third grade gifted and talented math students. *The National Research Center on the Gifted and Talented Newsletter*, 12–15. https://nrcgt.uconn.edu/newsletters/summer044

Matthews, D., Foster, J., Gladstone, D., Schieck, J., & Meiners, J. (2007). Supporting professionalism, diversity, and context within a collaborative approach to gifted education. *Journal of Educational and Psychological Consultation, 17*(4), 315–345. https://doi.org/10.1080/10474410701634161

Matthews, M. S. (2014). Advanced academics, inclusive education, and English language learning. In M. S. Matthews & J. A. Castellano (Eds.), *Talent development for English language learners: Identifying and developing potential* (pp. 1–14). Prufrock Press.

Matthews, M. S., & Castellano, J. A. (2014). *Developing English language learners' talents: Identifying and nurturing potential* [Webinar]. National Association for Gifted Children. https://www.nagc.org/demand-learning

McCoach, D. B. (n.d.). *Goal valuation: Valuing the goals of school.* https://nrcgt.uconn.edu/underachievement_study/goal-valuation/gv_section0

McGee, C., & Bowie, P. (2011). Section 1: Why start a parent group? In *Starting and sustaining a parent group to support gifted children* (pp. 8–10). National Association for Gifted Children.

Mofield, E. (in press). *What makes honors classes more than a name?* AMLE Magazine.

Mofield, E. (2014). *Instructional strategies for gifted students observation form.* Sumner County Schools.

Mofield, E. (2018). *Gifted education guide: Sequence of skills applied to advanced content.* Sumner County Schools.

Mofield, E. (2019). *Curriculum, planning, and instruction for gifted learners* [Conference session]. Kentucky Association for the Gifted Conference, Lexington, KY, United States.

Mofield, E. (2020a). *Bridging access to advanced content for diverse learners* [Conference session]. Partners in Education Conference, Nashville, TN, United States.

Mofield, E., & Parker Peters, M. (2018a). *Teaching tenacity, resilience, and a drive for excellence: Lessons for social-emotional learning for grades 4–8.* Prufrock Press.

Mofield, E., & Parker Peters, M. (2019). *Supporting gifted learners' potential by addressing underachievement* [Conference session]. Partners in Education Conference, Nashville, TN, United States.

Mofield, E. L. (2020b). Benefits and barriers to collaboration and co-teaching: Examining perspectives of gifted education teachers and general education teachers. *Gifted Child Today, 43*(1), 20–33. https://doi.org/10.1177/1076217519880588

Mofield, E. L., & Parker Peters, M. (2018b). Shifting the perfectionist's mindset: Moving toward mindful excellence. *Gifted Child Today, 41*(4), 177–185. https://doi.org/10.1177/1076217518786989

Montgomery, W. (2001) Creating culturally responsive, inclusive classrooms. *Teaching Exceptional Children 33*(4), 4–9. https://doi.org/10.1177/004005990103300401

Murawski, W. M. (2003). *Co-teaching in the inclusive classroom: Working together to help all your students find success.* Institute for Educational Development.

Murawski, W. A., & Lochner, W. W. (2018). *Beyond co-teaching basics: A data-driven, no-fail model for continuous improvement.* ASCD.

Murawski, W. M., & Spencer, S. A. (2011). *Collaborate, communicate, and differentiate! How to increase student learning in today's diverse schools.* Corwin.

National Association for Gifted Children. (n.d.). *Twice exceptionality* [White paper]. https://www.nagc.org/sites/default/files/Position%20Statement/twice%20exceptional.pdf

National Association for Gifted Children. (2019). *2019 Pre-K–Grade 12 Gifted Programming Standards.* http://www.nagc.org/sites/default/files/standards/Intro%202019%20Programming%20Standards.pdf

National Center for Research on Gifted Education. (2016). *Effective practices for identifying and serving English learners in gifted education: A systematic review of the literature.* https://ncrge.uconn.edu/wp-content/uploads/sites/982/2016/01/NCRGE_EL_Lit-Review.pdf

National Institute of Mental Health. (2018). *Anxiety disorders.* https://www.nimh.nih.gov/health/topics/anxiety-disorders/index.shtml

Norwood, K., & Burke, M. A. (2011). Education. In L. Wildflower & D. Brennan (Eds.), *The handbook of knowledge-based coaching: From theory to practice* (pp. 211–220). Jossey, Bass.

Novak, A. M. (2018). What works in professional learning for educators of the gifted: Findings from research and legislation. In A. M. Novak & C. L. Weber (Eds.), *Best practices in professional learning and teacher preparation: Methods and strategies for gifted professional development* (Vol. 1, pp. 5–22). Prufrock Press.

Oettingen, G., & Gollwitzer, P. M. (2010). Strategies of setting and implementing goals: Mental contrasting and implementation intentions. In J. E. Maddux & J. P. Tangney (Eds.), *Social psychological foundations of clinical psychology* (pp. 114–135). Guilford Press.

Olszewski-Kubilius, P., & Clarenbach, J. (2012). *Unlocking emergent talent: Supporting high achievement of low-income, high-ability students.* National Association for Gifted Children.

Park, G., Lubinski, D., & Benbow, C. P. (2007). Contrasting intellectual patterns predict creativity in the arts and sciences. *Psychological Science, 18*(11), 948–952. https://doi.org/10.1111/j.1467-9280.2007.02007.x

Paul, R., & Elder, L. (2019). *Critical thinking: Tools for taking charge of your learning and your life* (3rd ed.). Pearson.

Perkins, D. (2003). *King Arthur's round table: How collaborative conversations create smart organizations.* Wiley & Sons.

Peters, S. J., Matthews, M. S., McBee, M. T., & McCoach, D. B. (2013). *Beyond gifted education: Designing and implementing advanced academic programs.* Prufrock Press.

Phelps, V. (in press). Differentiation through independent study: The I-LEARN process. In A. Quinzio-Zafran & E. Wilkins (Eds.), *The new teacher's guide to overcoming common challenges: Curated advice from award winning teachers.* Routledge.

Phelps, V. (2020). *Addressing the needs of twice-exceptional learners template.* Sumner County Schools.

Plucker, J. A., & Peters, S. J. (2018). Closing poverty-based excellence gaps: Conceptual, measurement, and educational issues. *Gifted Child Quarterly, 62*(1), 56–67. https://doi.org/10.1177/0016986217738566

Powers, E. A. (2008). The use of independent study as a viable differentiation technique for gifted learners in the regular classroom. *Gifted Child Today, 31*(3), 57–65. https://doi.org/10.4219/gct-2008-786

Ramos, S. J. (2015). *Visualizing from within: A naturalistic inquiry on the implementation of mindsketching to build the academic literacy of children raised in poverty* [Unpublished doctoral dissertation]. Texas A&M University.

Reis, S. M., Baum, S. M., & Burke, E. (2014). An operational definition of twice-exceptional learners: Implications and applications. *Gifted Child Quarterly, 58*(3), 217–230. https://doi.org/10.1177/0016986214534976

Reis, S. M., & McCoach, D. B. (2000). The underachievement of gifted students. What do we know and where do we go? *Gifted Child Quarterly, 44*(3), 152–170. https://doi.org/10.1177/001698620004400302

Renzulli, J. S., & Reis, S. M. (2014). *The schoolwide enrichment model: A how-to guide for talent development* (3rd ed.). Prufrock Press.

Robbins, P. (1991). *How to plan and implement a peer-coaching program.* Association for Supervision and Curricular Development.

Roberts, J. (2017). Planning for advocacy. In R. D. Eckert & J. H. Robins (Eds.), *Designing services and programs for high-ability learners: A guidebook for gifted education* (2nd ed., pp. 200–211). Corwin.

Roberts, J. L., & Inman, T. F. (2015). *Assessing differentiated student products: A protocol for development and evaluation* (2nd ed.). Prufrock Press.

Robinson, A., Shore, B. M., & Enersen, D. L. (2007). *Best practices in gifted education: An evidence-based guide.* Prufrock Press.

Rock, D. (2008). SCARF: A brain-based model for collaborating with and influencing others. *NeuroLeadership Journal, 1,* 78–87.

Rubenstein, L. D., Siegle, D., Reis, S. M., McCoach, D. B., & Burton, M. G. (2012). A complex quest: The development and research of underachievement interventions for gifted students. *Psychology in the Schools, 49*(7), 678–694. https://doi.org/10.1002/pits.21620

Scruggs, T. E., Mastropieri, M. A., & McDuffie, K. A. (2007). Co-teaching in inclusive classrooms: A metasynthesis of qualitative research. *Exceptional Children, 73*(4), 392–416. https://doi.org/10.1177/001440290707300401

Shakenova, L. (2017). The theoretical framework of teacher collaboration. *Khazar Journal of Humanities and Social Sciences, 20*(2), 34–48. https://doi.org/10.5782/2223-2621.2017.20.2.34

Siegle, D. (2013). *The underachieving gifted child: Recognizing, understanding, and reversing underachievement.* Prufrock Press.

Siegle, D., & McCoach, D. B. (2005). Making a difference: Motivating gifted students who are not achieving. *Teaching Exceptional Children, 38*(1), 22–27. https://doi.org/10.1177/004005990503800104

Siegle, D., McCoach, B., & Gubbins, E. J. (2019). *Project BUMP UP: Building up mathematics proficiency utilizing push-in.* University of Connecticut, National Center for Research in Gifted Education.

Siegle, D., McCoach, D. B., & Roberts, A. (2017). Why I believe I achieve determines whether I achieve. *High Ability Studies, 28*(1), 59–72. https://doi.org/10.1080/13598139.2017.1302873

Slocumb, P., Payne, R., & Williams, E. (2017). *Removing the mask: How to identify and develop giftedness from students in poverty.* Aha Process.

Sorby, S., Casey, B., Veurink, N., & Dulaney, A. (2013). The role of spatial training in improving spatial and calculus performance in engineering students. *Learning and Individual Differences, 26,* 20–29. https://doi.org/10.1016/j.lindif.2013.03.010

Stambaugh, T. (2018). Curriculum and instruction within a talent development framework. In P. Olszewski-Kubilius, R. F. Subotnik, & F. C. Worrell (Eds.), *Talent development as a framework for gifted education: Implications for best practices and applications in school* (pp. 95–127). Prufrock Press.

Steele, C. M., & Aronson, J. (1995). Stereotype threat and the intellectual test performance of African Americans. *Journal of Personality and Social Psychology, 69*(5), 797–811. https://doi.org/10.1037/0022-3514.69.5.797

Stieff, M. (2013). Sex differences in the mental rotation of chemistry representations. *Journal of Chemical Education, 90*(2), 165–170. https://doi.org/10.1021/ed300499t

Taba, H., Durkin, M. C., Fraenkel, J. R., & NcNaughton, A. H. (1971). *A teacher's handbook to elementary social studies: An inductive approach* (2nd ed.). Addison-Wesley.

Tieso, C. (2004). Through the looking glass. One school's reflection. *Gifted Child Today, 27*(4), 58–62. https://doi.org/10.4219/gct-2004-155

Treffinger, D., & Isaksen, S. (2005). Creative problem solving: The history, development, and implications for gifted Education and talent development. *Gifted Child Quarterly, 49*(4), 342–353. https://doi.org/10.1177/001698620504900407

Treffinger, D. J., & Selby, E. C. (2009). Levels of Service (LoS): A Contemporary Approach to Programming for Talent Development. In J. S. Renzulli, E. J. Gubbins, K. S. McMillen, R. D. Eckert, & C. A. Little (Eds.), *Systems and models for developing programs for the gifted and talented* (2nd ed., pp. 629–654). Prufrock Press.

Tschannen-Moran, B., & Tschannen-Moran, M. (2011). The coach and the evaluator. *Educational Leadership, 69*(2), 10–16.

VanTassel-Baska, J. (2003). *Curriculum planning and instructional design for gifted learners.* Love.

VanTassel-Baska, J. (2015). Putting together the puzzle: The logic of design and development of curriculum for gifted learners. In H. E. Vidergor & C. Harris (Eds.), *Applied practice for educators of gifted and able learners* (pp. 77–86). Sense.

VanTassel-Baska, J. (2018). Achievement unlocked: Effective curriculum interventions with low-income students. *Gifted Child Today, 62*(1), 68–82. https://doi.org/10.1177/0016986217738565

VanTassel-Baska, J., & Baska, A. (2019). *Curriculum planning and instructional design for gifted learners* (3rd ed.). Prufrock Press.

VanTassel-Baska, J., & Stambaugh, T. (2006). *Comprehensive curriculum for gifted learners* (3rd ed.). Pearson.

Vygotsky, L. S. (1978). *Mind in society: The development of higher psychological processes.* Harvard University Press.

Webb, J., Amend, E., Webb, N., Goerss, J., Beljan, P., & Olenchak, F. R. (2005). *Misdiagnosis and dual diagnoses of gifted children and adults: ADHD, bipolar, OCD, Asperger's, depression, and other disorders.* Great Potential Press.

Weber, C. L., Behrens, W. A., & Boswell, C. (2016). *Differentiating instruction for gifted learners: A case studies approach.* Prufrock Press.

Weber, C. L., Boswell, C., & Behrens, W. A. (2014). *Exploring critical issues in gifted education: A case studies approach.* Prufrock Press.

West, L. (2009). Content coaching: Transforming the teaching profession. In J. Knight (Ed.), *Coaching approaches and perspectives* (pp. 145–165). Corwin.

WIDA Consortium. (2014). *The 2012 amplification of the English language development standards: Kindergarten–grade 12.* WIDA. https://wida.wisc.edu/sites/default/files/resource/2012-ELD-Standards.pdf

Wigfield, A., & Eccles, J. S. (2002). *Development of achievement motivation.* Academic Press.

Winner, E. (2009). Toward broadening our understanding of giftedness: The spatial domain. In F. D. Horowitz, R. F. Subotnik, & D. J. Matthews (Eds.), *The development of giftedness and talent across the life span* (pp. 75–86). American Psychological Association.

Zhao, Y., Pugh, K., Sheldon, S., & Beyers, J. L. (2002). Conditions for classroom technology innovations. *Teachers College Record, 104*(3), 482–515.

About the Authors

Emily Mofield, Ed.D., is an assistant professor in the College of Education at Lipscomb University, where she teaches gifted education and doctoral research courses. Her background includes 15 years' experience teaching gifted students and leading gifted services. Emily currently serves as the National Association for Gifted Children (NAGC) Chair for Curriculum Studies and has coauthored numerous award-winning gifted language arts curricula with Tamra Stambaugh (Vanderbilt Programs for Talented Youth). She is also the author/coauthor of several research publications related to perfectionism, achievement motivation, and collaborative teaching practices. Emily is the corecipient of the 2016 NAGC Hollingworth Award for excellence in gifted education research and the 2019 Texas Association for the Gifted and Talented Legacy Book Award for *Teaching Tenacity, Resilience, and a Drive for Excellence.* She is regularly invited to speak at conferences and school districts across the nation on social-emotional learning, curriculum, and differentiation for gifted learners.

Vicki Phelps, Ed.D., is lead consulting teacher for gifted education in Sumner County, TN. She has been involved in gifted education for the last 20 years, including collaboratively developing and opening a gifted magnet school and providing professional learning opportunities to schools and districts seeking to improve best practice in gifted education. Vicki is a National Board Certified Teacher and an active member in multiple gifted organizations. She is currently working on research publications focused on gifted adolescent motivation and regularly presents at state, national, and world gifted conferences. Vicki's work on differentiation will also be included in the upcoming book *The New Teacher's Guide to Overcoming Common Challenges: Curated Advice From Award-Winning Teachers.*